THE MOVIEGOER'S COMPANION

Rhiannon Guy

Introduction by Barry Norman

A THINK BOOK FOR

ROBSON BOOKS

No art passes our conscience in the way film does, and goes directly to our feelings, deep down into the dark rooms of our souls.

Ingmar Bergman

THINK
A Think Book
for Robson Books

First published in Great Britain in 2004 by
Robson Books
The Chrysalis Building, Bramley Road, London W10 6SP

An imprint of **Chrysalis** Books Group plc

Edited by Rhiannon Guy
The Companion team: Vicky Bamforth, James Collins, Harry Glass,
Emma Jones, Matthew Stadlen, Jo Swinnerton, Lou Millward Tait
and Malcolm Tait

Think Publishing
The Pall Mall Deposit
124-128 Barlby Road, London W10 6BL
www.thinkpublishing.co.uk

ISBN 1-86105-797-0

Printed and bound by Clays Ltd, Bungay, Suffolk NR35 1ED
The publishers and authors have made every effort to ensure the accuracy and
currency of the information in The Moviegoer's Companion. Similarly, every
effort has been made to contact copyright holders. We apologise for any
unintentional errors or omissions. The publisher and authors disclaim any
liability, loss, injury or damage incurred as a consequence, directly or
indirectly, of the use and application of the contents of this book.

The length of the film should be directly related to the endurance of the human bladder.

Alfred Hitchcock

A FIVE STAR REVIEW

This book would not have been possible without the research, ideas, and dogged support of:

Dominic Bates, Paul Bates, Adam Biles, Sarah Bove, Gemma Clunie, Stuart Fance, Kim Gifford, Lucy Grewcock, Ivo Grigorov, Angharad, Douglas and Kay Guy, Lisa Holm, Nikki Illes, Abi Moore, Charli Morgan, Naomi Pollard, Nathalie Stahelin, Jennifer Style and Toby Wagstaff.

The longest film ever made (it says here) ran for 87 hours and was called *The Cure for Insomnia*. I didn't see it, thank God, but I've seen many others that seemed as long and they were cures for insomnia, too.

The worst attempt at an accent (it also says here) was by Sean Connery trying to sound Irish in *The Untouchables*. Actually, I disagree – he wasn't trying to sound Irish at all; he was just being his Scottish self as always.

But that's the charm of this book: it's packed with quirky bits of incidental information and also arbitrary opinions with which you can cheerfully feel free to agree or disagree.

Glance inside and you will learn the name of the character Marilyn Monroe played in *The Seven Year Itch* – and I bet that will surprise you. You'll also discover the origin of popcorn and an explanation of all those credit titles you could never understand, like Best Boy and Dolly Grip and, no, Dolly Grip isn't the name of the female star's body double.

Whether you're a movie anorak or just somebody who likes films this book offers a wealth of stuff that will enlighten, amuse, possibly astonish and maybe even exasperate you. What more could you ask?

Barry Norman

The Lumière brothers, Louis (1864–1948) and Auguste (1862–1954)
First presented a short film to an audience in Paris in 1895. It was the first public presentation of a film and showed workers leaving the brothers factory for lunch. They invented the ciné-matographe: a machine that combined the functions of camera and projector and was thus able to project films onto a screen to an audience. The invention was patented on 13 February 1895 and within just two years, the Lumière catalogue included well over a thousand films, all of them single-shot efforts running under a minute.

Thomas Edison (1847–1931)
Inventor extraordinaire, Edison played a pivotal role in the development of cinema. It was he who suggested equidistant holes along the sides of cine film to regulate its flow through the camera. Some of the first moving pictures were made in his film studio. Before he died in 1931, Edison had registered 1,033 inventions at the US Patent Office.

Georges Méliès (1861–1938)
Méliès was a French magician who saw the Lumière brothers' first film. He introduced the concept of a story film, rather than just showing action. He is considered the father of special effects, built the first movie studio in Europe, and was the first person to use storyboards. He eventually produced over 500 films.

Edwin S Porter (1868–1941)
Porter was the first person to make films for the masses. He made the first Western, *The Great Train Robbery* (1903), which lasted 11 minutes. He also pioneered many modern cinema techniques including shooting films out of sequence so as to minimise moving between locations and switching the action from the train robbers to the forming of the posse.

Lee de Forest (1873–1961)
De Forest developed Phonofilm in 1923; a way to synchronise sound on film, which became the basis for the introduction of talking pictures in 1927. The first talkie was *The Jazz Singer* (1927) and was produced by Warner Brothers. The invention of sound for films saved Warner Brothers production company from going bankrupt.

QUOTE UNQUOTE

It is an axiom of cinema history, one admitting of few exceptions, that the longer the film's title the likelier it is to be an outright dud.
Gilbert Adair, US screen writer and critic

---

10 *Amount, in thousands of dollars, asked of any potential investor to help the funding of* The Thomas Crown Affair *(1999) in return for a bit part*

FORBIDDEN FILMS

Superstar: The Karen Carpenter Story (1987) a biography of Karen Carpenter, the easy-listening superstar who lost her battle against anorexia nervosa in 1983 at the age of 32. However, it was not that that got the film banned, but the fact that the film was made entirely using Barbie and Ken dolls. Richard Carpenter and Mattel both sued director Todd Haynes for illegally using Carpenters songs, and for using Mattel Barbie dolls in this film. Both cases were upheld, and it is now illegal to sell or distribute it in the US.

The Great Dictator (1940), written, directed and starring Charlie Chaplin, the film made fun of Hitler and Nazi Germany. Chaplin has said that if he had known the extent of Nazi atrocities, he could not have made fun of their homicidal insanity. However, when work on the film was started in 1937, the crimes of the Third Reich were not well known. The film was banned in Hitler's Germany and all Nazi occupied countries, although it is thought that Hitler himself saw the film twice. The film was also banned in Spain until dictator Francisco Franco died in 1975.

TAGLINE TEASERS

On which movie posters would you see these taglines?

1. Ever wanted to be someone else? Now you can.

2. Deadly. Silent. Stolen.

Answers on page 153.

MOVIE THERAPY

Seasoned filmgoers know all about the therapeutic effects of the cinema, but movie therapy takes their happiness a step further. Movie therapy was developed to help people access emotions through films because it was believed that people are more likely to respond to images and archetypal situations than to a therapist in an office. Films can act as a shortcut to self discovery because viewers can relate to the characters and situations they are shown. Different films work for different people, but an old favourite is *It's A Wonderful Life* (1946) which is apparently particularly good at calming people down. Attending movie therapy involves finding a film that matches your feelings and then watching the movie while paying close attention to your reactions to the film. You can then talk through the feelings with a professional. Be worried if you start feeling a strange link to Freddie Kruger.

Minimum age limit for ET – The Extra Terrestrial *(1982) in Sweden* **11**
after claims the film shows parents being unpleasant to children

HIGHEST EARNING SILENT FILMS
AT THE WORLDWIDE BOX OFFICE

1. *The Birth of a Nation* (1915)
2. *The Big Parade* (1925)
3. *Ben Hur* (1926)
4. *The Ten Commandments* (1923)
5= *The Covered Wagon* (1923)
5= *What Price Glory* (1926)
7= *Hearts of the World* (1918)
7= *Way Down East* (1921)
9= *The Four Horsemen of the Apocalypse* (1921)
9= *Wings* (1927)

DREAM SEQUENCE

Self help for movie buffs

Watching a film
If you dream that you are watching a film, this could mean that you are watching life pass you by. To help interpret this dream, try and notice how the film parallels situations in your own life and how the characters might reflect your own life or character. Watching a film can also signify that you are analysing yourself without being emotionally attached. If you are waiting for the film to start, that might suggest you are not sufficiently involved in life.

Starring in a film
This dream signifies that something from your unconscious is soon to emerge. To dream of yourself in a film can also represent memories or scenes from your past, or a new role that you are about to take on in life.

Being in a cinema
Dreaming of being in a cinema can mean that you are trying to protect yourself from your emotions or actions. Viewing difficult situations on the big screen helps to distance you from emotional damage.

The baddie
If you dream about a film villain it is likely to be a reflection of you thinking about starting a dangerous activity or vice.

QUOTE UNQUOTE

*A young girl travels to a psychedelic landscape where
she kills the first person she meets, then teams up with
three complete strangers to kill again.*
TV Guide preview of *The Wizard of Oz*

January 1976. 'Tonight at the London Film-makers Co-op Cinema, a rare screening of David Larcher's extraordinary *Monkey's Birthday*. Be there or be square.' Well, let no one call me square, so on the stroke of six I switched off my typewriter, fixed my make up and set off from the office for Camden Town, clacking across the courtyard in my high heels to the cinema.

This was the cinema? An icy concrete room in what had previously been a piano factory. Rows of directors' chairs already filled with regular patrons who were sensibly equipped with rugs, blankets, primus stoves and thermos flasks of hot soup. I seemed to be the only one not wearing baggy dungarees, scarf, woolly hat and mittens.

'How long is the film?'

'Six hours'

I wrapped my coat around me and huddled in the canvas chair. The film began: it had no conventional plot or dialogue, but instead an ever more complex series of ravishing abstract colours and grainy textured footage of deserts filmed in shimmering heat. Even so it was difficult to suspend disbelief; after two hours my toes were numb and my teeth began to chatter. Another hour passed and my limbs were rigid. On screen vivid flashing colours alternated with dark shadows, like a light being switched on and off. I started to join in, squinting, opening my eyes wide, then watching with each eye alternately open or closed. But when I closed my left eye all I could see with my right was a black screen with a pinpoint of light in one corner, and after a time I realised that this did not correspond with the film. Either it was an optical illusion or something was badly wrong with my right eye.

The following day found me at Moorfields Eye Hospital; it wasn't an optical illusion.

Felicity Sparrow in *Seeing in the Dark:*
A Compendium of Cinemagoing

COUNTRIES WITH THE
MOST CINEMA SCREENS IN 2001

1. China	65,500
2. USA	36,764
3. India	11,962
4. France	5,236
5. Germany	4,792
6. Spain	3,770
7. UK	3,248
8. Italy	3,050
9. Canada	2,900
10. Japan	2,585

The 'Rat Pack' was the name given to a group of select friends of Frank Sinatra who performed and partied with him in the early 1960s.

Rat Pack was supposedly a name that Lauren Bacall used to describe a group of Humphrey Bogart's drinking friends. The name stuck to Sinatra and his allies.

The Pack's pinnacle of fame came in 1960, when the group arrived in Las Vegas to make the film *Ocean's Eleven*. The group filmed during the day and performed two live shows nightly at the Sands Casino.

The Rat Pack were:

Frank Sinatra was 44 when he filmed *Ocean's Eleven*. In his career he won a best supporting actor Oscar in 1954 for *From Here To Eternity* (1953) and was also awarded an honorary Oscar in 1971. He starred in dozens of films, was married four times and in 1970 won the Hersholt Humanitarian Academy Award. The epitaph on his headstone reads 'The best is yet to come'.

Dean Martin was 43 when *Ocean's Eleven* was filmed. He made 51 films in his career, is one of the only people to have two stars on the Hollywood Walk of Fame, one for films and one for television. He died in 1995 on Christmas Day, the same day as his mother, but 29 years later.

Sammy Davis Jr was 35 for *Ocean's Eleven*. He lost his left eye in a car crash and was reputed to smoke four packs of cigarettes every day. He converted to Judaism in the mid 1960s and married a white woman in 1960, courting huge controversy as his actions were considered risqué at the time.

Joey Bishop had been a stand-up comic before *Ocean's Eleven* when he was 42. He wrote much of the material that the Rat Pack performed on stage but usually played the straight man. He also appeared on television many times and was guest host on *The Tonight Show* 177 times, more than any one else.

Peter Lawford was married to Patricia Kennedy during the Rat Pack's peak years. She was the sister of John F Kennedy and so facilitated the friendship between Sinatra and JFK. Lawford was married four times, was 37 at the time of *Ocean's Eleven*, and visited Marilyn Monroe the night she died with his brother in law, Robert Kennedy. He was also the only member of the Rat Pack to be British and was considered the heart throb of the group with his accent and silver hair.

Ocean's Eleven was remade in 2001 by director Steven Soderbergh, with George Clooney, Brad Pitt and Julia Roberts. With the exception of the title character 'Danny Ocean', none of the principal characters have the same names as their counterparts in the 1960 version of the film.

14 *Number of Hollywood films directed by women between 1949 and 1979; in the same period, men directed 7332*

She made him an omelette he couldn't refuse.

THE CRITICAL LIST

Pauline Kael (1919–2001)

Kael acquired national fame and notoriety during the late 1960s and 1970s, when she became one of the central critics of art and 'auteur cinema' (films by a director that collectively establish his personal style and views). She is best known for her enduring 'The Current Column' in The New Yorker, where she worked from 1968 to 1991. She wrote several successful books *I Lost it at the Movies* (1954) and *Kiss Kiss Bang Bang* (1965) and had short appearances in several movies, including *A Soldier's Daughter Never Cries* (1998) alongside Woody Allen.

Kael was renowned (and feared) for her brash, unpredictable reviews and her ability to remember even the smallest details about the films she saw. In 1966 she was fired from *McCall Magazine* for slaughtering *The Sound of Music* (1965) and calling it 'The Sound of Mucus'. And in 1979 she controversially accepted a job as executive consultant at Paramount Pictures. Kael retired from writing when she was diagnosed with Parkinson's disease. The Paulettes (as her fans have been nicknamed) remain a growing and active circle even after her death.

Number of films in the top 20 films at the UK box office that were made 15
in the US in 2003

The house lights went down; fiery letters stood out solid and as though self-supported in the darkness. THREE WEEKS IN A HELICOPTER. AN ALL-SUPER-SINGING, SYNTHETIC-TALKING, COLOURED, STEREOSCOPIC FEELY. WITH SYNCHRONISED SCENT-ORGAN ACCOMPANIMENT.

'Take hold of those metal knobs on the arms of your chair' whispered Lenina. 'Otherwise you won't get any of the feely effects.'

The savage did as he was told.

Those fiery letters, meanwhile, had disappeared; there were ten seconds of complete darkness; then suddenly, dazzling and incomparably more solid-looking than they would have seemed in actual flesh and blood, far more real than reality, there stood the stereoscopic images, locked in one another's arms, of a gigantic Negro and a golden-haired young brachycephalic Beta-Plus female.

The savage started. That sensation on his lips! He lifted a hand to his mouth; the titillation ceased; he let his hand fall back on the metal knob; it began again. The scent organ, meanwhile, breathed pure musk. Expiringly, a second-track super-dove cooed 'Oo-ooh', and vibrating only thirty-two times a second, a deeper than African bass made an answer: 'Aa-aah.' 'Ooh-ah! Ooh-ah!' the stereoscopic lips came together again, and once more the facial erogenous zones of the six thousand spectators in the Alhambra tingled with almost intolerable galvanic pleasure. 'ooh...'

Aldous Huxley, *Brave New World*

CRINGING OSCAR MOMENTS

In a cringeworthy opening number, Rob Lowe was forced to sing 'Proud Mary' while dancing with an actress dressed as Snow White at the 1989 award ceremony. Disney was so distressed that it threatened to sue over the misuse of their character.

A number of actresses have become somewhat emotional during their acceptance speech but Anna Paquin went further and nearly hyperventilated after winning best supporting actress for *The Piano* (1993). However, she was only 12 at the time.

Richard Gere suggested the audience send telepathic love to Deng Xiaoping, the leader of China who was responsible for human rights abuses in China and Tibet, so that he might let the people live in freedom.

Marlon Brando sent Sacheen Littlefeather to pick up the trophy in 1973 for his best actor role in *The Godfather* to protest at Hollywood's treatment of American Indians. She was later exposed as not being native American but an actress from California.

KEEP IT IN THE FAMILY

An Ideal Husband (1999)
Father of the Bride (1950 and 1991)
The Butcher's Wife (1991)
All About My Mother (1999)
Jesus' Son (1999)
The General's Daughter (1999)
O Brother, Where Art Thou? (2000)
Two Mules for Sister Sara (1970)
Uncle Buck (1989)
Along Came Auntie (1926)
My Cousin Vinnie (1992)
Granny Get Your Gun (1940)

FILM CLASSIFICATION

Since 1913 the British Board of Film Classification has decided film ratings in the UK. However the decision to release a film lies with local councils who also decide what age groups can be admitted. In practice the councils nearly always abide by the BBFC's certificates.

When it comes to videos, the BBFC have had legal powers since 1985 (previously there were no video ratings) and are obliged to rate every new video release. The ratings determine the age a person needs to be to buy and rent a video.

1913–1932
U (Universal) – Suitable for children
A (Adult) – Some councils ruled that children must be accompanied by an adult

2002
Uc (Universal Children) – Suitable for all, but especially suitable for young children to watch on their own (video only)
U (Universal) – Suitable for all
PG (Parental Guidance) – All ages admitted, but parents are advised that certain scenes may be unsuitable for small children
12A (12 Accompanied) – Suitable for those aged 12 and over, but under 12s may be admitted if they are accompanied by an adult (cinema only)
12 – Suitable for those aged 12 and over (video only)
15 – Suitable for those aged 15 and over
18 – Suitable for those aged 18 and over
R18 (Restricted 18) – Suitable for those aged 18 and over and only available at licensed cinemas and shops. Yes that does mean sex shops.

LONGEST FILMS EVER SCREENED

Film	Country	Year	Duration
1. *The Cure for Insomnia*	USA	1987	87hrs
2. *The Longest and Most Meaningless Movie in The World*	UK	1970	48hrs
3. *The Burning of the Red Lotus Temple*	China	1931	27hrs
4. *Die Zweite Heimat*	West Germany	1992	25hrs 32mins
5. **** (aka 'Four Stars')	USA	1967	25hrs
6. *Heimat – Eine deutsche Chronik*	West Germany	1984	15hrs 40mins
7. *Berlin Alexanderplatz*	West Ger/Italy	1980	15hrs 21mins
8. *Resan* ('The Journey')	Sweden	1987	14hrs 33mins
9. *Comment Yukong Deplaca les Montagnes* ('How Yukong Moved the Mountains')	France	1976	12hrs 43mins
10. *Out 1: Noli me Tangere*	France	1971	12hrs 9mins

COLLECTIVELY

While a group of actors is referred to as a company, a group of critics is known as a 'shrivel'.

BRIT BAD GUYS

When Hollywood needs a bad guy, they often choose an Englishman. Alan Rickman, for example, has done rather well out of embracing the role of British villain in *Robin Hood: Prince of Thieves* (1991) where he hammed it up and won a BAFTA for his efforts. And in *Die Hard* (1988) he takes on a German accent (another bad guy favourite) for Hans Gruber. Jeremy Irons followed in Rickman's bad shoes by playing his brother, Simon Gruber, in *Die Hard: With A Vengeance* (1994).

Gary Oldman has also had his share of bad guy roles. Although he rarely actually plays a Brit, he is often first on the bad guy casting list. He went for the ham approach in *Leon* (1994) as bad cop Norman Stansfield; in *The Fifth Element* (1997) he played the evil Jean-Baptiste Emanuel Zorg; in *True Romance* (1993) he played Drexl Spivey; and in *Air Force One* (1997) he played the Russian Ivan Korshunov.

HAPPY HOUR

Film: *The Seven Year Itch* (1955)

Plot: Richard Sherman finds himself alone in New York during the summer while his wife and son enjoy the country. He intends to work and keep out of any trouble. Unfortunately for him a voluptuous blonde (Marilyn Monroe) moves in upstairs. And one who is fond of dipping potato chips in champagne.

Quote: Richard Sherman: There's gin and vermouth. That's a martini.
Girl: Oh, that sounds cool! I think I'll have a glass of that. A big tall one!

Recipe:
Whiskey Sour
2 oz bourbon
Juice of 1/2 lemon
1/2 tsp powdered sugar
1 cherry
1/2 slice lemon

Shake the bourbon, juice of lemon, and powdered sugar with ice together. Strain the mixture into a whiskey sour glass and decorate with the slice of lemon, top with the cherry, and serve.

QUOTE UNQUOTE

Every great film should seem new every time you see it.
Roger Ebert, US film critic

SIGNS THAT YOU GO TO
THE CINEMA TOO OFTEN

- You consider popcorn to be a major food group
- You can predict which film the trailers are advertising in less than 10 seconds
- You recite the legal disclaimer at the end of films
- You have become accustomed to drinking from containers the size of buckets
- You know the ushers by name
- You know the cinema company's jingle off by heart
- You have a favourite seat at the cinema and get upset when someone else is sitting there
- Half your monthly income goes on cinema tickets
- You consider seeing films more important to your well being than say, eating
- You have developed the ability to see in the dark

WORDS ON FILM

Some of my foster families used to send me to the movies to get me out of the house, and I'd sit all day and way into the night... I loved anything that moved up there and I didn't miss anything that happened – and there was no popcorn either!

Marilyn Monroe, *Marilyn in Her Own Words*

THEY SHOULD HAVE STAYED AT HOME

The Passion of the Christ (2003)

A 57-year-old woman passed out during the crucifixion scene in *The Passion of the Christ* and later died at hospital. Peggy Law Scott was watching the film in Wichita in Kansas in the USA. Following the craze for *en masse* visits by church congregations, a Brazilian pastor booked a whole cinema for his congregation. Unfortunately 43-year-old Jose Geraldo Soares suffered a heart attack during the film and died. However, his wife who was sitting beside him denies that the film's violent scenes caused him to die. She said he had been enjoying the film.

MOST RENTED VIDEOS IN THE UK

Four Weddings and a Funeral (1994)
Dirty Dancing (1987)
Basic Instinct (1992)
Crocodile Dundee (1986)
Gladiator (2000)
Sister Act (1992)
Forrest Gump (1994)
The Sixth Sense (1999)
Home Alone (1990)
Ghost (1990)

THE BIG FIVE

Only three films have won all five of the key Academy Awards of best picture, best director, best actor, best actress and best screenplay:

It Happened One Night (1934)
Frank Capra, Clark Gable, Claudette Colbert, Robert Riskin

One Flew Over the Cuckoo's Nest (1975)
Milos Foreman, Jack Nicholson, Louise Fletcher, Lawrence Hauben, Bo Goldman

The Silence of the Lambs (1991)
Jonathan Demme, Anthony Hopkins, Jodie Foster, Ted Tally

20 *Height, in metres, of the British Film Industry London IMAX cinema screen the largest in the UK*

A ROGUE'S GALLERY OF DISNEY VILLAINS

The Queen in *Snow White and the Seven Dwarfs* (1937) – the first cartoon thought suitable to be preserved by the National Film Preservation Board.

Captain Hook in *Peter Pan* (1953) – as is the tradition in the stage performance, the same actor does the voice for Mr Darling and Captain Hook.

Ursula in *The Little Mermaid* (1989) – Ursula was based on the actor Harris Glen Milstead who made his name as the comic and outrageous transvestite Divine.

Stepmother in *Cinderella* (1950) – her voice was provided by Eleanor Audley who also voiced **Maleficent** in *Sleeping Beauty* (1959). The sound department asked the US Army to provide some training videos on flame throwing to capture the sound of Maleficent's fiery breath when she turns into a dragon.

Cruella de Vil in *101 Dalmatians* (1961) – de Vil was reportedly based on the actress Tallulah Bankhead.

Prince John in *Robin Hood* (1973) – the cowardly prince was voiced by Peter Ustinov.

Jafar in *Aladdin* (1992) – Disney considered Jafar to be a classic Disney villain, reminiscent of their early films.

Shere Khan in *The Jungle Book* (1967) – the voice of the tiger was provided by George Sanders who announced his intention to commit suicide when older in 1937. He did so in 1972.

Scar in *The Lion King* (1994) – the menacing lion was voiced by Jeremy Irons. The scar on Scar's face is in exactly the same place as it is on Al Pacino's character Tony Montana in the movie *Scarface* (1983).

STUDIO SUMMARIES

Columbia Pictures

Logo: a young woman wearing a toga and holding up a torch

Key facts: Columbia Pictures was founded in 1924 by Harry Cohn, and was first known as CBC Film Company. It remains unclear which model posed for the logo, although several actresses claim to be the figure in question. Since the appearance of Lady Columbia has changed over time (at first she was dark haired, draped in an American flag, then her hair became fairer and the flag turned blue) it is possible that several models were used. In 1993 she became dramatically slimmer and her torch a lot dimmer as part of a 'return to the classic look'. Columbia's more recent box office successes include *Gandhi* (1982), *Men in Black* (1997) and *Spider-Man* (2002).

WHAT'S IN A NAME?

Film stars and their real names

Alan Alda	Alphonso Joseph d'Abruzzo
Woody Allen	Allen Stewart Konigsberg
Fred Astaire	Frederick Austerlitz
Lauren Bacall	Betty Joan Perske
Anne Bancroft	Anna Maria Louisa Italiano
Tony Bennett	Antonio Dominic Benedetto
Dirk Bogarde	Derek Jules Gaspard Ulric Niven van den Bogaerde
Charles Bronson	Charles Buchinsky
Albert Brooks	Albert Einstein
Mel Brooks	Melvin Kaminsky
Nicholas Cage	Nicholas Coppola
Michael Caine	Maurice J Micklewhite
Cher	Cherilyn Sarkisian
Joan Crawford	Lucille LeSueur
Tom Cruise	Thomas Cruise Mapother IV
Tony Curtis	Bernard Schwartz
Doris Day	Doris Kappelhof
Bo Derek	Mary Cathleen Collins
Kirk Douglas	Issur Danielovitch Demsky
Douglas Fairbanks Jr	Douglas Elton Ulman Jr
Judy Garland	Frances Gumm
Cary Grant	Archibald Alexander Leach
Rita Hayworth	Margarita Cansino
Rock Hudson	Roy Scherer
Boris Karloff	William Henry Pratt
Michael Keaton	Michael Douglas
Ben Kingsley	Krishna Bhanji
Stan Laurel	Arthur Stanley Jefferson
Bruce Lee	Lee Yuen Kam
Sophia Loren	Sophia Scicoloni
Chico Marx	Leonard Marx
Groucho Marx	Julius Marx
Gummo Marx	Milton Marx
Harpo Marx	Adolph Marx
Zeppo Marx	Herbert Marx
Jack Palance	Vladimir Palanuik
Ginger Rogers	Virginia Katherine McMath
Mickey Rooney	Joe Yule Jr
Winona Ryder	Winona Horowitz
Jane Seymour	Joyce Penelope Wilhelmina Frankenberg
Omar Sharif	Michael Shalhoub
Charlie Sheen	Carlos Irwin Estevez
Martin Sheen	Ramon Estevez

22 *Number, in millions, of bees used in* The Swarm *(1978), the largest cast of animals used in any film*

PARROTS OF THE CARIBBEAN

Captain Jack Sparrowlegs

QUOTE UNQUOTE

Cinema managers are nice and let you pop in to see a film without telling. My mother has seen quite a few films that way recently.
Princess Anne

TAGLINE TEASERS

On which movie posters would you see these taglines?

1. Living with a roommate can be murder.

2. In space no one can hear you scream.

Answers on page 153.

Robin Williams

When Williams won the academy award for best supporting actor in *Good Will Hunting* (1997), he sent Peer Augustinski, who is his German dubbing voice, a miniature Oscar replica with a note saying 'Thank you for making me famous in Germany.'

Giancarlo Giannini

After Giannini dubbed Jack Nicholson's voice in the Italian version of *The Shining* (1980), he received a telegram of congratulations from Stanley Kubrick for successfully capturing the difficult performance.

Oreste Lionello

Lionello is a famous Italian comic who has also found fame as the dubbing voice for Woody Allen, who enjoys a large following in Italy. Most foreign films are dubbed in Italy and moviegoers have often never heard an actor's real voice. For many Italians, Lionello's voice is Woody Allen's voice.

Kristin Scott Thomas

Thomas speaks French fluently and so was able to dub herself in French in *Four Weddings and a Funeral* (1994).

Yvan Attal

The French actor and director dubbed Tom Cruise's voice for the French releases of *Eyes Wide Shut* (1999), *Mission: Impossible II* (2000) and *Vanilla Sky* (2001). He is married to the actress Charlotte Gainsborough, daughter of the singer Serge Gainsborough and actress Jane Birkin.

CONFUSED IN TRANSLATION

Translations of film titles into the local lingo can often leave English speakers baffled, amused or both. Titles are often changed to give the local audience a better understanding of what the film is about, as many Western titles don't travel well. For example, in America a film was released in 1992 called *Encino Man*. However, British audiences will probably only know it as *California Man*. Because few Brits know that Encino is a city in California. When films are sold to the Far East, the translations can become even more obscure. Such as:

Nixon (1995) became *The Big Liar*
Boogie Nights (1997) became *His Powerful Device Makes Him Famous*
Fargo (1996) became *Mysterious Murder in Snowy Cream*. The words 'snowy cream' are pronounced 'fah go'.
Leon (1994) became *This Hit Man Is Not as Cold as He Thought*
As Good As It Gets (1997) became *Mr. Cat Poop*

In 1998 Bruce Willis turned up with fifty minutes or so of *Armageddon*, an apocalyptic yarn about a comet threatening to destroy Earth. This footage was to be shown at a cinema in Cannes, by invitation only, to an audience of international critics and journalists. At the appointed hour we duly assembled, took our seats and waited. And waited. People as lofty as Bruce Willis cannot be expected to turn up on time. Punctuality is for peasants. A good twenty minutes went by before Willis, the director Michael Bey and various acolytes made their grand entrance and the screening began. All went well for a bit. This was not an inspired film but it seemed workmanlike enough until they showed us the great emotional climax – the scene in which the noble Willis, having landed on the comet, is about to blow up both himself and it to save the world but before doing so is somehow linked by satellite with his daughter, Liv Tyler, back on Earth. This is the last time they will ever talk to each other; she will never see her daddy again. Tear-jerking stuff and it duly evoked tears – of mirth. The audience burst into a spontaneous howl of joy, crying with laughter, rocking in their seats.

Willis was furious. 'I didn't realise we'd made a comedy,' he said in a brief and surly speech on the stage. Nor was his mood any better the next day when people were taken to the Hotel du Cap to interview him. Instead of making light of yesterday's mild disaster, perhaps admitting that the scene might have looked odd when taken out of context but insisting that it would be terrific in the finished film – in other words, showing a sense of humour, which would have endeared him to all – he behaved as if those of us who had laughed at his big emotional moment were guilty of *lèse-majesté* at the very least. He cut interviews down to a point where some people were only allowed two minutes in his presence, went off for a long and leisurely lunch, insisted that critics didn't matter because nobody read them anyway, so sucks boo, and generally behaved like a spoilt little boy who had been told that, no, he couldn't have any sweeties because they would spoil his appetite. It was wonderful; all of us who went to Cap that day agreed Willis was a fairly considerable plonker.

Barry Norman, *And Why Not? Memoirs of a film lover.*

QUOTE UNQUOTE

If you suck on a tit the movie gets an R rating.
If you hack the tit off with an axe it will be PG.
Jack Nicholson, US actor

Frank could be just as ruthless with scripts. During an afternoon shoot, he invited me for a drink in his trailer. The assistant director came to the trailer to call us to set.

'We're having a drink,' said Frank, 'because it's 'tini time.'

'But, Mr. Sinatra,' protested the assistant director, 'we are behind schedule and we need to make up time.'

'How far behind are we?' asked Frank.

'Two weeks,' answered the assistant director.

'Say, buddy. You have a script handy?' asked Frank.

I knew what was coming.

The assistant director handed him his script. Frank counted off about twenty pages and then ripped them out of the script.

'There, pal,' he said. 'Now we're on schedule.'

The assistant director fled, not wanting to put us ahead of schedule. The pages never went back in. It was just like Frank. When he went on record that something was over, it was over. The writers had to piece the story together somehow. Frank realised later he had cut one of my big scenes, so he threw the end of the picture to me.

'Let the kid get in the way of the bullet,' he said to Sol Siegel. 'That'll make the audience feel sorry for her because she tried to save my life. Might get her a nomination out of it.'

He was right. I got my first Academy Award nomination for *Some Came Running*. I wondered what would have happened had he wanted two or three martinis that day.

Shirley MacLaine, *My Lucky Stars*

QUOTE UNQUOTE

All I need to make a comedy is a park, a policeman and a pretty girl.
Charles Chaplin, film actor and director

FORBIDDEN FILMS

The Rocky Horror Picture Show (1975), based on the hit musical, was banned in Singapore for nearly 30 years because of its sexual and masochistic content. Eventually the movie made its debut there in 2003, but only people over 21 years old were allowed to watch it.

The Roman epic *Ben Hur* (1925) was banned in China in 1930 for containing 'propaganda of superstitious beliefs, namely Christianity.'

Zoolander (2001) is banned in Malaysia because of a story line in which a fictional Malaysian Prime Minister is the subject of an assassination attempt.

CRINGING OSCAR MOMENTS

In 1974 while David Niven was presenting an award, a streaker ran across the stage. Niven managed to recover the moment by ad libbing the line: 'The only laugh that man will ever get in his life is by stripping ...and showing his shortcomings.'

In her infamous speech, Sally Field uttered the words 'You like me – you really like me' when she accepted the best actress award for *Places in the Heart* (1984). Despite being apparently overwhelmed by the occasion, she had actually already won a best actress award for her role in *Norma Rae* (1979).

Not exactly the picture of modesty, James Cameron declared to the world 'I'm the king of the world' in his acceptance speech for the best director of *Titanic* (1997), mimicking Leonardo Di Caprio's line from the film. He then asked everyone to observe a minute's silence for all the people who lost their lives when the Titanic went down in 1912.

Not content with winning the best supporting Oscar for *City Slickers* (1992), 72-year-old Jack Palance further proved he could compete with his younger co-nominees by spontaneously doing one-arm press ups on stage.

10 GREATEST FILM HEROES

Atticus Finch in *To Kill a Mockingbird* (1962)
Indiana Jones in *Raiders of the Lost Ark* (1981)
James Bond in *Dr. No* (1962)
Rick Blaine in *Casablanca* (1942)
Will Kane in *High Noon* (1952)
Clarice Starling in *The Silence of the Lambs* (1991)
Rocky Balboa in *Rocky* (1976)
Ellen Ripley in *Aliens* (1986)
George Bailey in *It's a Wonderful Life* (1946)
TE Lawrence in *Lawrence of Arabia* (1962)

In a ballot held by the American Film Institute in 2003 the greatest heroes were selected by a panel of distinguished members of the film community, from directors, screenwriters, actors, editors, cinematographers, visual effects artists, stunt men and women and make-up artists.

MIXED-UP MOVIE STARS

Unscramble these famous actors
AUTUMN HARM • I WARM BILLIONS
ANORAK'S IN TOWN
Answer on page 153.

Number of people thanked by Olivia de Havilland when she won best actress 27 for To Each His Own *(1946). She holds the Guinness World Record*

'Come on with the rain, I've a pine on my face.'

QUOTE UNQUOTE

*If I find a film dull, I find it infinitely more entertaining
to watch the scratches.*
Norman McLaren, UK film maker

28 *Year, in the twentieth century, when a lavatory bowl was first shown in a film
(The Crowd)*

FUNNY FILM PORN TITLES

**Porn film titles that take their
inspiration from actual films:**

Intercourse with the Vampire
The Sperminator
Muffy the Vampire Layer
Sperms of Endearment
Romancing the Bone
Clockwork Orgy
Sex Trek: The Next Penetration
Doctor Yes
A League of Their Moan
Single Tight Female
Sleazy Rider
Shaving Ryan's Privates
Wet Dream on Elm Street
Bonfire of the Panties
White Men Can't Hump
Whore of the Roses
Good Will Humping
ET – The Extra Testicle
Inspect Her Gadget

MOVIE DOUBLE ACTS

Fred and Ginger

Fred Astaire (1899–1987). The evaluation of Astaire's first screen test: 'Can't act. Can't sing. Balding. Can dance a little.'

Buried at Oakwood Memorial Park, Chatsworth, California, USA, the same cemetery as Ginger Rogers.

Ginger Rogers (1911–1995). Although Astaire usually got top billing, Ginger Rogers was quoted as saying: 'I did everything Fred Astaire did, and I did it backwards and in high heels.'

Fred and Ginger Films
Flying Down To Rio (1933)
The Gay Divorce (1934)
Roberta (1935)
Top Hat (1935)
Follow the Fleet (1936)
Swing Time (1936)
Shall We Dance (1937)
Carefree (1938)
The Barkleys of Broadway (1949)

Hollywood has a reputation for short and multiple marriages. Some people go the extra yard and make plans for 'until death do us part' over and over again.

Elizabeth Taylor has been married eight times. Two of her unions were with actor Richard Burton who she was married to between 1964 and 1974 and again between 1975 and 1976. Seven of her marriages ended in divorce although one of her husbands died in a plane crash on a plane called 'The Lucky Liz'. She has been unmarried since 1996 but has four children and nine grandchildren.

Although not a prolific or well-respected actress, **Zsa Zsa Gabor** is well remembered for her multiple trips up the aisle. Among her husbands are hotelier Conrad Hilton, actor George Sanders and her current beau Prince Frederick von Anhalt who brings the total to nine. They have been married since 1986.

One of the classic film stars of the 1940s and 1950s, **Lana Turner** was also fond of marriage. She was married seven times, twice to Steve Crane. Her daughter from that marriage, Cheryl Crane, killed Johnny Stompanato, Lana's lover, between two of her marriages. The killing was later determined to be a justifiable homicide.

Former child star **Mickey Rooney** has been married since 1978 to January Chamberlin but, before her, he was married seven times. His most famous bride was Ava Gardner (who had also been married to Frank Sinatra). One of his wives, Carolyn Mitchell, was murdered by her lover in 1966 who then committed suicide.

HITCHCOCK'S BLONDES

Ingrid Bergman	*Spellbound* (1944)
	Notorious (1945)
	Under Capricorn (1949)
Grace Kelly	*To Catch a Thief* (1955)
	Rear Window (1954)
	Dial M For Murder (1954)
Janet Leigh	*Psycho* (1960)
Kim Novak	*Vertigo* (1958)
Eve Marie Saint	*North By Northwest* (1959)
Tippi Hedren	*The Birds* (1963)
	Marnie (1964)

Some of the longest ever film titles

- *The Saga of the Viking Women and their Voyage to the Waters of the Great Sea Serpent* (1957)
  Sometimes shortened to the *Saga of the Viking*.

- *Oh Dad, Poor Dad, Mamma's Hung You in the Closet and I'm Feelin' so Sad* (1967)

- *The Persecution and Assassination of Jean-Paul Marat as Performed by the Inmates of the Asylum of Charenton Under the Direction of the Marquis de Sade* (1967)
  Usually abbreviated to *Marat/Sade*.

- *The Incredibly Strange Creatures Who Stopped Living and Became Mixed-Up Zombies* (1967)
  The title was originally going to be *The Incredibly Strange Creature: Or Why I stopped Living and Became a Mixed-up Zombie*, but Columbia Pictures threatened writer/director/star Ray Dennis Steckler with a massive lawsuit, thinking that the title was too similar to their upcoming Stanley Kubrick film, *Dr Strangelove: Or How I Learned to Stop Worrying and Love the Bomb*. Steckler was amazed that Columbia would feel so threatened by his little $38,000 film. He phoned the studio to straighten things out, but couldn't make any progress until he demanded that Kubrick get on the line. Then Steckler simply suggested the new title – Kubrick accepted, and the whole thing was dropped.

- *Can Hieronymus Merkin Forget Mercy Humppe and Find True Happiness?* (1969)

- *You've Got to Walk it if you Like to Talk it or You'll Lose that Beat* (1971)

- *Who is Harry Kellerman and Why is he Saying Those Terrible Things About Me?* (1971)
  It has the longest title of any film ever nominated for an Academy award – best supporting actress for Barbara Harris.

- *The Adventures of Buckaroo Banzai across the 8th Dimension* (1984)

- *Night of the Day of the Dawn of the Son of the Bride of the Return of the Revenge of the Terror of the Attack of the Evil, Mutant, Alien, Flesh Eating, Hellbound, Zombified Living Dead Part 2: In Shocking 2-D* (1991)
  Usually abbreviated to *Night of the Day of the Dawn of the Son of the Bride of the Return of the Terror*.

MAFIA CONNECTIONS

The Mafia has been a favourite of filmmakers for decades. Just think of *The Godfather* series (1972, 1974 and 1990), *Good fellas* (1990), *Road to Perdition* (2002) and as far back as *Scarface* (1932), which was later to be remade in 1983 with Al Pacino. So it is perhaps not surprising that some actors have been rumoured to be involved with 'La Cosa Nostra.' The most famous suspect was Frank Sinatra who was accused of achieving his success because of his 'links' with organised crime. Sinatra always denied it, but the authorities kept an eye on him all the same. His FBI file was 2,403 pages long, even though he was never charged with a mafia-related crime. Despite never officially being linked to the mob, he is widely thought to be the basis for the character of Johnny Fontane

in *The Godfather* (1972). Ex-wife Mia Farrow states in her autobiography that he offered to have Woody Allen's legs broken when Allen was found to be having an affair with her adopted daughter Soon-Yi Previn.

A less well-known actor, George Raft, was also widely believed to have Mafia connections. He used the reputation to his advantage in *Scarface* (1932), but eventually the alleged connection led to the decline of his career.

In 2000, Steven Seagal testified against Anthony 'Sonny' Ciccone for allegedly demanding the actor pay back money to his former agent who was a friend of the crime family. Seagal also said that he was told to make movies with the men – or else. Some might say demanding that Steven Seagal be in any films is a crime in itself.

HAPPY HOUR

Film: *Withnail and I* (1987)

Plot: Not so much cocktail aficionados as professional drunks, Withnail and 'I' decide to take a holiday to escape from their dreary London life.

Quote: Withnail [having just drunk a bottle of lighter fluid]: 'Got any more?'

I: 'No. I have nothing.'

Withnail: 'Liar. What's in your toolbox?'

I: 'Nothing.'

Withnail: 'Liar. You've got antifreeze.'

I: 'You bloody fool. You should never mix your drinks.'

Richard E Grant played the dedicated drinker Withnail but is a teetotaller in real life. While shooting he decided to get drunk once, just to be able to identify with the character. Not one to do things by halves he washed down a large helping of vodka. The cast and crew have said that Grant may never be as funny as he was that day.

WORDS ON FILM

When we attended film shows in the RAF the national anthem was played *before* the picture, accompanied by film footage of the Queen riding side saddle down Horse Guards Parade. We had wagers on how many times the horse's prick bounced back and forth in the time it took to cross the Parade. Arguments were fierce: some said six, some six and a half, some seven. As we all stood to attention in the darkened cinema, singing the anthem, we would count them off: 'God save our – one – gracious Queen – two – Long live our – three – noble Queen – four.'

Alf MacGabhan in *Seeing in the Dark:
*A Compendium of Cinemagoing***

QUOTE UNQUOTE

Film is one of the three universal languages,
the other two: mathematics and music.
Frank Capra, US film director

CRINGING OSCAR MOMENTS

At the first Oscar festivities, in 1934, host Will Rogers announced the winner for Best Director by exclaiming, 'Come up and get it, Frank!' A jubilant Frank Capra (*Lady for a Day*) began his trip to the podium. Unfortunately, the real winner was Frank Lloyd (*Cavalcade*). Capra called his return to his table, 'The longest, saddest, most shattering walk in my life.'

In 1985, Sir Laurence Olivier, the Shakespearean actor, was asked to present the award for best picture. However the 78-year-old forgot to name any of the best picture nominees. He simply opened the envelope and proclaimed, 'Amadeus!'

In 1971 George C Scott became the first actor to refuse an Oscar. He won the best actor award for his role in *Patton* but did not attend the awards ceremony and refused the award, saying that 'The (Academy Awards) ceremonies are a two-hour meat parade, a public display with contrived suspense for economic reasons.' He stayed at home and watched an ice hockey game on television.

In 1994, Tom Hanks won his first Oscar for a poignant and groundbreaking role as a lawyer dying of AIDS in *Philadelphia*. He gave a heart-felt speech, in which he famously thanked his gay high-school drama teacher. The only problem was that the teacher had not yet come out. The gaffe inspired the comedy *In & Out* (1997) with Kevin Kline, in which Matt Dillon 'outs' his teacher while accepting an Academy Award.

THE CRITICAL LIST

Gene Siskel (1946–1999)

Eugene Siskel was one half of famous film critic duo Siskel and Ebert. Siskel graduated from Yale in 1967 and started his career working for the *Chicago Tribune* in 1969. In 1974, he was teamed up with Roger Ebert and together they devised a method of rating films as either 'thumbs-up or thumbs-down'. Their system became famed and a 'thumbs-up' decision on a film was soon a gateway to box office success. Siskel died in 1999 after complications from surgery to remove a brain tumour.

Siskel's favourite film was *Saturday Night Fever* (1977). He also owned the white suit John Travolta wore in the film, having bought it at a charity auction.

In an interview, Siskel said that if he were trapped on a desert island and could watch only one film, that film would be *2001: A Space Odyssey* (1968).

Roger Ebert (1942–)

Roger Ebert is best known for his partnership with fellow critic Gene Siskel and their 'thumbs-up, thumbs-down' ratings system. He also wrote the screenplay for the 1969 cult film, *Beyond the Valley of the Dolls* directed by Russ Meyer.

Ebert considers the worst film he has ever seen to be *I Spit On Your Grave* (1978).

His right thumb is trademarked.

He owns a life-sized statue of Oliver Hardy.

He once said in an interview that if he were trapped on a desert island and could watch only one film, that film would be *Citizen Kane* (1941).

Ebert estimates that he has seen over 8,000 films in his lifetime.

SWEAR IT AGAIN

The 1983 film *Scarface* starring Al Pacino held the record for using the most swear words (206) until *Goodfellas* overswore it with 246 in 1990. Four years later, *Pulp Fiction* breezed past it with 257 of the rudest swear words. The clear winner, however, is *South Park: Bigger, Longer and Uncut* (1999), which holds the title with 399. As well as using the word 'fuck' 133 times, the film also features 128 offensive gestures and 221 acts of violence.

The brains behind *South Park* are Matt Stone and Trey Parker who brought *South Park* to the world as a cartoon series on television. Not a cartoon for children; the programme has generated huge opposition because of its 'challenging' subject matter and prolific swearing.

ANOTHER DIMENSION

3-D films create the illusion that images are jumping out from the screen towards the audience. This is achieved by taking two pictures using two identical cameras placed side by side. When the two images are placed together each eye only sees the image taken on the same side as the eye. This is interpreted in the viewer's brain as a three-dimensional image.

The movie industry first used the technique in 1915 in a short film called *Jim, the Penman*. It was shown in New York but the trend didn't catch on. However, directors sporadically made 3-D films, even if the audiences were not particularly interested in them. That all changed in the early 1950s with the release of *Bwana Devil* (1952), directed by Arch Oboler and produced by Sidney W Pink. Pink shot the film by using a film with two lenses and is considered the father of the genre. He went on to produce over 50 3-D films during the 1950s. In one scene, the film depicts lions eating British railway workers in Kenya. Reports from the time indicate that the public were more than happy to be scared by the three-dimensional lions leaping out at them out of the screen. And, of course, the added amusement of wearing green and red glasses was all part of the fun.

The craze for 3-D cinema continued throughout the 1950s but the films lost favour when viewers began to get headaches from watching the films and 2-D showed itself to be out selling 3-D. Alfred Hitchcock made *Dial M For Murder* (1954) in 3-D but it was swiftly followed by a more conventional 2-D release. There were some attempts to revive the form in later years once the genre was less popular, but 3D films never regained the appeal of the 1950s. That said, many current IMAX films are made in 3-D.

ONE WANTS A BIGGER TRAILER

While the royal family's screen appearances have mostly been limited to news reports and the Queen's Speech on Christmas Day, a couple of royal personages have made it on to the big screen. Edward VIII (while Prince of Wales) appeared in the *Power of Right* (1919) and *The Warrior Strain* (1919). There was then a long pause in royal film appearances until Prince Charles became the first member of the royal family to speak in a fiction film (made for video) called *Grime Goes Green: Your Business and the Environment* (1990). The film was co-written by John Cleese.

GREEN IS GOOD

Actors who have turned green to get the part

Margaret Hamilton (1902–1985) The cackling Wicked Witch of the West from *The Wizard of Oz* (1939). Margaret originally trained as a nursery school teacher and was devoted to children. The Oz role almost cost her life when she was badly burned during one of the early scenes. She was supposed to disappear into a puff of smoke, but her make-up caught fire. She was absent from the set for more than a month before recovering and returning to complete her role as the witch.

Jim Carrey (1962–) In *The Mask* (1994), Carrey played Stanley Ipkiss who became a charismatic and irresistible wild man when he put on a magical mask. With the mask he was able to woo Cameron Diaz and save the day from a criminal gang.

Carrey also gave in to green in *How The Grinch Stole Christmas* (2000). The film was a big screen adaptation of the classic story told by Dr Seuss and saw Carrey wearing a full green and hairy body suit.

Willem Dafoe (1955–) became the Hollywood version of the comic book villain the Green Goblin in *Spider-Man* (2002).

Eric Bana (1968–) became comic book character the Incredible Hulk in *Hulk* (2003). Ang Lee created the green one using CGI technology.

FAMILY TIES

Some lesser-known film relationships:

Christopher Lee is the cousin of Ian Fleming
Rita Hayworth is the cousin of Ginger Rogers
Francis Ford Coppola is the uncle of Nicolas Cage
Olivia de Havilland is the sister of Joan Fontaine
Ingrid Bergman is the mother of Isabella Rossellini
Tippi Hedren is the mother of Melanie Griffith
Angelina Jolie is the daughter of Jon Voight

QUOTE UNQUOTE

It was once argued that 'Starring Sylvester Stallone' were the three scariest words in the English language but until I saw Adam Sandler, I'd always thought the three scariest words in the English language were 'starring Dan Aykroyd'.
Joe Queenan, US writer and film reviewer

CONTINUOUS COMPLICATIONS

Continuity errors are usually the result of multiple takes being made of one scene when, by the 26th take, no one notices that an open door is now closed, or the leading man's shirt has changed colour. But while continuity errors can ruin a film, they would nonetheless be very useful in real life.

Five continuity errors everyone would like in real life

Drinks that refill
Clocks that never move forward
Self-healing wounds
Self-tidying hairstyles
Self-cleaning houses
Self-ironing clothes

STUDIO SUMMARIES

Paramount Studios

Logo: a snow-covered mountain and a ring of stars.

Key facts: Founded on 8 May 1912 by WW Hodkinson, Paramount introduced the 'block booking system', which meant that to show a popular film, exhibitors had to buy a whole package of films, usually containing one blockbuster and several B-movies. Paramount dominated the market as it was the first nationwide distributor and had most major stars under contract including American sweetheart Mary Pickford and Douglas Fairbanks.

ALL DAY AT THE MOVIES

Dawn of the Dead (1978 and 2004)
Daylight (1996)
Morning Departure (1950)
Breakfast at Tiffany's (1961)
High Noon (1952)
Naked Lunch (1991)
Dog Day Afternoon (1975)
Sunset Boulevard (1950)
Twilight for the Gods (1958)
The Evening Star (1996)
A Night at the Opera (1935)
Midnight Cowboy (1969)

Young Indiana Bones

WORDS ON FILM

Maybe I just didn't have the temperament for stardom. I'll never forget seeing Bette Davis at the Hilton in Madrid. I went up to her and said, 'Miss Davis, I'm Ava Gardner and I'm a great fan of yours.' And do you know, she behaved exactly as I wanted her to behave. 'Of course you are, my dear,' she said.' Of course you are.' And she swept on. Now that's a star.

Ava Gardner, *My Story*

BUZZ WORDS

The word 'paparazzi' is derived from the name of a character in Federico Fellini's *La Dolce Vita* (1960). The lead character in the film, Marcello, has a friend who photographs celebrities. His name was Paparazzo, the plural is paparazzi and so the phrase was born. The term also bears a resemblance to the Sicilian word for an oversized mosquito, *papataceo*, which for Fellini adequately summed up the parasitical nature of the photographers and journalists in the film.

TAGLINE TEASERS

On which movie posters would you see these taglines?

1. The man with the hat is back.
And this time, he's bringing his Dad.

2. Being the adventures of a young man whose principal interests
are rape, ultra-violence and Beethoven.

Answers on page 153.

TOP TEN MOVIE MONSTERS

As voted by readers of *Empire Magazine* in 2004

1. **King Kong** (*King Kong*, 1933)
2. **Talos** (*Jason and the Argonauts*, 1963)
3. **The Alien** (*Alien*, 1979)
4. **The T-Rex** (*Jurassic Park*, 1993)
5. **The Thing** (*The Thing*, 1982)
6. **Shelob** (*Lord of the Rings: The Return of the King*, 2003)
7. **The Metaluna Mutant** (*This Island Earth*, 1955)
8. **Tetsuo** (*Akira*, 1988)
9. **The Skinned Werewolf** (*The Company of Wolves*, 1984)
10. **The Troll** (*Harry Potter and the Philosophers Stone*, 2001)

I'D LIKE TO THANK...

BAFTAS

The British Academy Film and Television Awards (BAFTA) began in 1946 when Alexander Korda formed a club for the most eminent people in the British film world. Korda himself was already Sir Alexander, as in 1942 he had become the first film personality to be knighted.

The club was formed at the Hyde Park Hotel, under the chairmanship of David Lean and with the contribution of Carol Reed and Charles Laughton.

The first statuettes, of a bronze, seated lady, were designed by sculptor Henry Moore and were worth £550. The current statues were designed in 1955 by Mitzi Cunliffe. The statue is based on a traditional mask but the reverse of the mask has an electronic symbol round one eye and a screen symbol around the other linking dramatic production and television technology.

The first film to win the BAFTA film award was *The Best Years of Our Lives* (1946) at the 1947 ceremony.

CRITICS WHO GOT IT WRONG

Film: *Silence of the Lambs* (1990)
Review: 'Preposterous fantasy' – Stuart Klawans, *Nation*.
Facts: The third ever film to win the 'big five' at the Oscars: best picture, best director, best screenplay, best actor (Anthony Hopkins) and best actress (Jodie Foster.) It grossed almost $150 million in the US and the UK alone.

Film: *Apocalypse Now (*1979)
Review: 'A very ugly, very minor work' – *Atlanta Journal*.
Facts: Nominated for eight Oscars, it won two for cinematography and sound. Consistently listed as one of the greatest films of all time.

Film: *Star Wars* (1977)
Review: 'As exciting as last year's weather reports' – John Simon, *New York Post*.
Facts: Nominated for 10 Oscars, it won six for best art direction/set decoration, best costume, best visual effects, best film editing, best original score and best sound. It is the 12th biggest grossing movie of all time taking $797,900,000. It was voted the best film of all time in a Channel 4 poll in 2001.

Film: *Taxi Driver* (1976)
Review: 'A rambling, unfocused, one-dimensional wallow in cheap sensationalism' – Marcia Magill, *Films in Review.*
Facts: Nominated for four Oscars. Voted the 22nd best film of all time by viewers of Channel 4 in 2001.

Film: *Psycho* (1960)
Review: 'Hitchcock is not an entertainer, but a panderer of vicarious perversion' – Robert Hatch, *Nation*.
Facts: Nominated for four Oscars. Alfred Hitchcock was nominated as best director six times in his life and in 1968 won a special lifetime achievement award.

Film: *The Seven Year Itch* (1955)
Review: 'Monroe has been profoundly miscast' – Delmore Schwartz, *New Republic*.
Facts: The image of Monroe holding down her white dress as she stands over a subway grating has become one of the most recognised of the twentieth century.

Film: *ET – The Extra Terrestrial* (1982)
Review: 'As vulgar as a Brooke Bonds' TV chimps commercial' – *Time Out*.
Facts: Nominated for nine Oscars, it won for best sound effects editing, best visual effects, best original score and best sound. It is considered a children's classic and still shown regularly on television.

Film: *The Way We Were* (1973)
Review: 'Were Miss Streisand to collide with a Mack truck, the truck would drop dead' – *Esquire*.
Facts: Nominated for six Oscars (including best actress for Barbara Streisand), it won two for best original score and best original song.

THE LAST WORD

Film stars' last words…

My fun days are over.
US film star James Dean

Adieu my friends, I go to glory.
Dancer and actress Isadora Duncan

On the whole, I'd rather be in Philadelphia.
US comedian WC Fields

I want the sunlight to greet me.
Film star Ruldolph Valentino

I've had a hell of a lot of fun and I've enjoyed doing it.
US actor Errol Flynn

I am leaving you with your worries, good luck.
British actor George Sanders

I can't live any longer with my nerves.
US film star Jean Seberg

RECURRING NUMBERS

Stephen King seems to have found an affinity with the number 237. In the film *Stand By Me* (1986), based on a King novel, the boys raise $2.37 when they pool their money together. In *The Shawshank Redemption* (1994), based on a King short story, Red's cell number is 237. And in *The Shining* (1980) the hotel room is 237. However the director of the film, Stanley Kubrick, changed the room number from 217 (as specified in King's novel) because the staff feared no one would ever stay in room 217 again, whereas there was no room 237.

INTERIOR DECORATION: THE MOVIE

Forty-eight-year-old Derek Atkins has visited the Odeon cinema in York eight times a week since 1988. However he goes not to watch the films, but to study the décor. Atkins once worked as an usher and projectionist but now pays for the pleasure of simply sitting inside the cinema.

'It's very rare I actually watch the films, as I like to scrutinise the interior of the building and make mental notes for research purposes', says Atkins. 'I can tell instantly if there is a chip out of the paint.'

Atkins has visited all 97 Odeon cinemas in Britain and pays an annual visit to the grave of Odeon founder, Oscar Deutsch. He is planning to write a book about his fascination.

U-571 WHO

The depiction of history in any film is fraught with problems, not least because one person's fact is another's heavily biased fiction. *U-571* (2000) depicted the capturing of the Enigma coding machine from a German U-boat during World War Two, which was a major turning point in the war. However, the film showed the US Navy to be the captors rather than the Royal Navy. This reinterpretation of historical fact caused uproar in Britain and questions were raised in Parliament. Prime Minister Tony Blair agreed that the film was 'an affront to memories of the British sailors who lost their lives on this action'. Following the disgruntled reception in Britain, a caption was added to the film before the credits, outlining that the Royal Navy captured the first Enigma machine. The historical inaccuracy didn't bother the cinema-going public too much though; the film stayed in the box office top 10 for a month and reached a high of number four in the UK.

10 MOST PASSIONATE FILMS

1. *Casablanca* (1942)
2. *Gone with the Wind* (1939)
3. *West Side Story* (1961)
4. *Roman Holiday* (1953)
5. *An Affair to Remember* (1957)
6. *The Way We Were* (1973)
7. *Doctor Zhivago* (1965)
8. *It's a Wonderful Life* (1946)
9. *Love Story* (1970)
10. *City Lights* (1931)

In a ballot held by the American Film Institute in 2002, the most passionate films were selected by a panel of distinguished members of the film community, from directors, screenwriters, actors, editors, cinematographers, visual effects artists, stunt men and women and make-up artists.

FÜHRER'S FILMS

When the Allies reached Berlin in 1945 they found two films in Hitler's bunker; the German made *Der Hund von Baskerville* or 'The Hound of the Baskervilles' (1936) and *Der Mann, der Sherlock Holmes War* or 'The Man Who Was Sherlock Holmes' (1937). Sir Arthur Conan Doyle was obviously a favourite of the Führer. *Der Hund von Baskerville* has not survived the ages as a film masterpiece, possibly because it depicts Sherlock Holmes as a Nazi.

42 *Number of full-length feature films created by Walt Disney Feature Animation, as of 2002*

We were making it at the Goldwyn Studios off Formosa and Melrose, and the men's stuff was going to be easy. It was the ladies stuff that had me worried. Billy brought in a female impersonator to work with Jack and me and teach us things like how to hold our hands. If we held them up, our muscles showed. If we held them palm down, the muscles disappeared. When we walked in heels, we threw our weight forward and our bottoms under. We had our legs and chests shaved, eyebrows plucked, extensive makeup tests with lipstick and eyelashes and a variety of wigs with different cuts and colours. Our hips were padded underneath the dresses. We had a voice coach to help us pitch our voices higher.

To find the appropriate bra was no easy matter. I'm a 36D myself. The woman I was to be, I decided was a little bit of Grace Kelly for the debutante look, ZaSu Pitts for comedy style, and, of course, my darling mother for heart. After four or five days of makeup and hair and wardrobe tests, I told Jack, 'Listen, I'm sorry but you don't make a good-looking woman.' He was ugly as a woman. I was a little more attractive, but that's genetics. Anyway, we were sitting in my dressing room, and I said to Jack, 'We may look good on set, but how do we look in real life?'

'I don't know'

'Well, why we don't we test it? Let's go to the ladies room.'

'I don't think I want to do that.'

'Come on, let's just try it out.'

So we marched down past the commissary, into the ladies room, and went right to the mirrors. There were a couple of women standing around. I immediately took out my lipstick and started putting it on, watching the women coming in and out. The girls would come out of the stalls, come up behind us, fix their makeup, wash their hands – not one of them gave us a second look. When we got out of the ladies room, Jack said, 'We made it,' I said, 'No, we're just so ugly, they don't even see us.'

So we went back to the makeup men, Emil Levine and Henry Rae, and said, 'Guys, you gotta make us better-looking. Figure something out.' They gave us a little more eye shadow and a little more mascara, and we put on three-inch heels instead of the two-inch ones we were wearing. I had my busts enlarged. Jack had his waist pulled in. Back to the ladies room we went. And as soon as we walked in there, a girl said, 'Hi, Tony.'

I said, 'Let's go Jack.' That pretty much settled which makeup was better.

Tony Curtis, *The Autobiography*

QUOTE UNQUOTE

Cinema should make you forget you are sitting in a theatre.
Roman Polanski, Polish film director

FAMOUS ONE-LINERS

Clint Eastwood: 'Go ahead, make my day.'
Magnum Force (1973) and *Sudden Impact* (1983)

Clark Gable: 'Frankly, my dear, I don't give a damn.'
Gone With the Wind (1939)

Arnold Schwarzenegger: 'I'll be back.'
The Terminator (1984) and *Terminator 2: Judgement Day* (1991)

Humphrey Bogart: 'Here's looking at you, kid.'
Casablanca (1942)

Jack Nicholson: 'You can't handle the truth.'
A Few Good Men (1992)

Cuba Gooding Jr: 'Show me the money!'
Jerry Maguire (1996)

Richard E Grant: 'We want the finest wines available to
humanity, we want them here and we want them now.'
Withnail and I (1987)

Michael Caine: 'You were only supposed to blow the bloody
doors off!' *The Italian Job* (1969)

Robert De Niro: 'You talkin' to me?' *Taxi Driver* (1976)

Robert Duvall: 'I love the smell of napalm in the morning.'
Apocalypse Now (1979)

Estelle Reiner: 'I'll have what she's having.'
When Harry met Sally... (1989)

Anthony Hopkins: 'I do wish we could chat longer. But I'm having
an old friend for dinner.'
The Silence of the Lambs (1991)

Terry Jones: 'He's not the Messiah – he's a very naughty boy.'
Life of Brian (1979)

STUDIO SUMMARIES

Dreamworks SKG

Logo: a child sitting on the rim of a half moon, casting a fishing line.

Key facts: Steven Spielberg, Jeffrey Katzenberg and David Geffen were already extremely successful film makers when they founded their own studio in October 1994. Spielberg had directed several blockbusters, Katzenberg was the former head of animation at Disney Studios and David Geffen was the founder of Geffen Records. In its short history, Dreamworks has already produced 44 feature films including *Shrek* (2001) and *American Beauty* (1999).

---

44 *Calibre of the Magnum that accidentally killed Brandon Lee while filming*
The Crow (1994)

FILM AA

They played alcoholics:

Meg Ryan in *When A Man Loves A Woman* (1994)
Jack Lemmon and Lee Remick in *Days of Wine and Roses* (1962)
Nicolas Cage in *Leaving Las Vegas* (1995)
Sandra Bullock in *28 Days* (2000)
Dudley Moore in *Arthur* (1981)
Ed Harris in *Pollock* (2000)
Ray Milland in *The Lost Weekend* (1945)
Mickey Rourke in *Barfly* (1987)

They were alcoholics:

Oliver Reed
WC Fields
Errol Flynn
Peter O'Toole
Anthony Hopkins
Liza Minnelli
Luis Buñuel
Tallulah Bankhead
Buster Keaton
Verne Troyer

QUOTE UNQUOTE

*Scientists are complaining that the new Dinosaur movie shows
dinosaurs with lemurs, who didn't evolve for another million years.
They're afraid the movie will give kids a mistaken impression. What
about the fact that the dinosaurs are singing and dancing?*
Jay Leno, US talk-show host

MOVIE URBAN LEGENDS

Charlie Chaplin

Legend: Charlie Chaplin once lost a Charlie Chaplin look-alike
contest.

True. Chaplin was hugely popular in the early twentieth century
and his fame gave rise to a number of Chaplin look-alike
competitions. The aim was to capture the tramp character that
Chaplin portrayed on the big screen around 1915. Chaplin entered
one of these competitions in a theatre in San Francisco and failed
to even make the finals. The great silent movie star was reportedly
distressed at the inability of any of the other contestants to perfect
his distinctive walk.

The weight in pounds of the gold and white beaded gown worn by Sharon 45
Stone in Casino *(1995)*

GOING OUT IN STYLE

A random selection of violent and gory film deaths

Decapitation
Final Destination (2000): a character's head is cut off by a flying hubcap
Final Destination 2 (2003): a character gets her head stuck in a lift door which then goes up, decapitating her in the process
Freddy vs Jason (2003): Jason severs a character's head with his machete
Sleepy Hollow (1999): many different characters lose their heads at the hands of the headless horseman

Blendering
Gremlins (1984): a gremlin is dropped into a blender
Raiders of the Lost Ark (1981): a Nazi is thrown into a plane propeller
On Her Majesty's Secret Service (1969): a villain skis into a snow blowing machine
Fargo (1996): someone is thrown into a wood chipper

Slicing
Cube (1997): a character is sliced into small cubes and slowly disintegrates
Equilibrium (2002): a character's face is sliced by a sword and slowly slides off
Final Destination 2 (2003): a character gets hit by a flying piece of barbed wire fence, slicing him into several chunks.
Ghost Ship (2002): cruise ship patrons are sliced in half by

fast-moving wire
Highlander (1986): a villain's neck is severed, but the head remains in place long enough for the villain to chuckle
Kill Bill Vol. 1 (2003): the top of O-Ren Ishii's head is sliced off with a sword
Resident Evil (2002): a character is sliced into two small cubes by a moving grid of laser beams
Rob Roy (1995): a character gets cleaved by a sword and slowly peels in half
The Meaning of Life (1983): a soldier is sliced in half by a sword
Thirteen Ghosts (2001): a character is trapped between glass doors when they slam shut and when they open, half of him slides off the other.

Eaten
Jaws (1975): several characters eaten by sharks
Jurassic Park (1993): several characters eaten by dinosaurs
Snatch (2000): co-star eaten by starved pigs

Organs ripped out while alive
Hannibal (2001): a character sliced open and pushed over the balcony with his intestines tied to it.
Indiana Jones and the Temple of Doom (1984): a sacrificial victim's heart is ripped out
Merry Christmas Mr. Lawrence (1983): ritual disembowelling

We'll always have Parrots.

CUTTING OUT THE CUTS

Most film 'takes' last less than a minute, although good editing can make them seem longer. Director Sergio Leone broke the rules with his long sweeping shots that lasted several minutes. But in 2001, the Russian director Alexander Sokurov took the art of the long take to the next level. In the film *Russian Ark*, actors re-enact 300 years of Russian history, while the camera roams through 33 rooms of the Hermitage Museum in St Petersburg to the music provided by three live orchestras. All of it, right down to the roll of the last credit line, was shot in one single, continuous take.

The single-shot film was recorded straight into digital format because the conventional celluloid rolls are simply not long enough to shoot a 90-minute continuous take. There were three previous attempts to complete the film when the take was hindered by technical difficulties but the fourth and final attempt was a success.

FILMS WITH TITLES DERIVED
FROM SONG TITLES

Film	Song	Film
American Pie	1972	1999
Sweet Home Alabama	1976	2002
Bad Boys	1983	1995
Sea of Love	1959	1989
One Fine Day	1963	1996
My Girl	1965	1991
Something to Talk About	1991	1995
When a Man Loves a Woman	1966	1994
The Crying Game	1964	1992
Addicted to Love	1986	1997
Jumpin' Jack Flash	1968	1986
Keeping the Faith	1984	2000
Girls Just Want to Have Fun	1983	1985

TAGLINE TEASERS

On which movie posters would you see these taglines?

1. Off the record, on the QT, and very hush-hush...

2. Mischief. Mayhem. Soap.

Answers on page 153.

MOVIE DOUBLE ACTS

Jay and Silent Bob

This New Jersey slacker duo appear in almost every Kevin Smith film. Kevin Smith takes on the role of the mostly mute Bob, and Smith's old friend Jason Mewes plays Jay, who more than compensates for his friend's reticence.

Silent Bob speaks a total of 26 words in *Clerks* (1994)
Silent Bob speaks a total of eight words in *Mallrats* (1995)
Silent Bob speaks a total of 430 words in *Chasing Amy* (1997)
Silent Bob speaks a total of three words in *Dogma* (1999)
Silent Bob speaks a total of 102 words in *Jay and Silent Bob Strike Back* (2001)

QUOTE UNQUOTE

I've spent several years in Hollywood, and I still think the movie heroes are in the audience.
Wilson Mizner, US Screenwriter

TOO YOUNG

The huge hit *Monsters, Inc* (2001) featured the screen debut (well the voice) of Mary Gibbs as Boo (also known as Mary), the child that monsters Sulley and Mike inadvertently allow to enter their world. Mary was two and a half when she recorded her dialogue. In true diva style she refused to sit down and read the script. To solve this problem, the sound crew decided to follow her around as she went about her business and capture anything she might utter, gurgles, tantrums and all. They then found suitable sounds to fit the script.

COCKNEY SPARROWS

Film stars who are part of the rhyming slang dictionary:

Tommy Steele, *eel*

Richard Todd, *cod*

David Bowie, *blowy (ie windy)*

Michael Caine, *pain*

Oliver Reed, *weed (ie tobacco)*

Frankie Vaughan, *prawn*

Gregory Peck, *cheque*

Jane Russell, *mussel*

Doris Day, *way*

Dudley Moore, *sore*

Mickey Rooney, *loony*

WORDS ON FILM

Holly Golightly voices her opinion of the movie industry:

'He's still harping?' she said, and cast across the room an affectionate look at Berman. 'But he's got a point I should feel guilty. Not because they would have given me the part or because I would have been good: they wouldn't and I wouldn't. If I do feel guilty, I guess it's because I let him go on dreaming when I wasn't dreaming a bit. I was just vamping for time to make a few self-improvements: I knew damn well I'd never be a movie star. It's too hard; and if you're intelligent, it's too embarrassing. My complexes aren't inferior enough: being a movie star and having a big fat ego are supposed to go hand-in-hand and; actually, it's essential not to have any ego at all. I don't mean I'd mind being rich and famous. That's very much on my schedule, and some day I'll try to get around to it; but if it happens, I'd like to have my ego tagging along. I want to still be me when I wake up one fine morning and have breakfast at Tiffany's.'

Truman Capote, *Breakfast At Tiffany's*

*Age of film director William Desmond Taylor when he was murdered in   49
1922. His unsolved murder was the biggest scandal of the time*

The Madness of King George

Legend: The title of the 1995 British film 'The Madness of George III' was changed to *The Madness of King George* by its distributors in case American audiences thought it was the third installment of a 'Madness of George' film series.

Although the rumour about the film was enjoyed by many and widely circulated, it has been declared that the name of the film was not different in America and the rest of the world as the distributors have no power to change the name of the title. The film, however, was based on a play which was entitled *The Madness of George III*. The title was changed for the film partly because, as the director Nicholas Hytner has explained, the cultural differences between the US and Britain may mean that while a British audience would naturally assume that 'George III' referred to the Hanoverian monarch, an American audience might not make the same connection. However there was no consideration that US audiences might assume they had missed earlier films in a series.

TOP 10 MOST SUCCESSFUL FILMS
BASED ON TRUE STORIES

1.	*Titanic*	1997
2.	*Pearl Harbor*	2001
3.	*Apollo 13*	1995
4.	*Pocahontas*	1995
5.	*Catch Me if You Can*	2002
6.	*The Perfect Storm*	2000
7.	*Schindler's List*	1993
8.	*A Beautiful Mind*	2001
9.	*Chicago*	2002
10.	*Erin Brockovich*	2000

NEVER WORK WITH ANIMALS

Despite the old adage, director Michael Anderson employed the largest animal cast ever used on a film in *On Around the World in Eighty Days* (1956). Ninety animal handlers were needed to control the record number of 855 animals. The menagerie included 3,800 sheep, 2,448 buffalo, 950 donkeys, 800 horses, 512 monkeys, 17 bulls, 15 elephants, six skunks, and four ostriches.

I waited around in an agony of apprehension till finally, I was sent for to do the scene. Santell was kindness and patience itself and walked me gently through many rehearsals but I still couldn't relax.

This was my big chance but I was rigid with terror.

'Okay, Dave, let's take a crack at it – do it just like that last rehearsal – that was just fine.'

Miserable and sweating, I stood outside the door and listened to the happy sounds of the party inside. After an eternity, a red light glowed – my signal to burst in.

I did. My toe caught in the track and I nearly fell over. I bumped a dowager in a chair; I spilled somebody else's drink and said all the wrong lines to the wrong people but somehow, I staggered through to the end.

Everyone on set applauded.

I couldn't believe my ears. Santell rushed up.

'Hey, that's great, Dave! Just what I wanted…perfect! Now we have that one in the can we'll just take another for safety…Oh! This time don't hit the track, and watch out for the old dame's chair…one or two little changes…just clean it up a little…but it's great and we have it already – this one's a luxury.'

I stood outside the door looking at that red light…I couldn't wait for it to go on. 'This is easy,' I thought, 'this is fun!'

I sailed through the second take, loving every minute of it, completely relaxed.

At the end of the day, Stuart Hall and I were celebrating in a bar: he told me the secret. Santell had addressed the whole 'set' while I had been shivering and shaking in my dressing room.

'The boy who's playing Leo – this is his first big scene in a picture and we've all got to help him loosen up. After the first take, however bad he is, I want you all to applaud, then I'll put some film in the camera.'

Santell is in my private Hall of Fame.

David Niven, *The Moon's A Balloon*

STUDIO SUMMARIES

Universal Studios

Logo: a rotating globe, although different versions have been used (flaming, frozen, metallic, etc.)

Key facts: Founded in 1912 by German immigrant Carl Laemmle, Universal Studios made its name (but not a lot of money) by producing early horror classics *Dracula* (1931), *Frankenstein* (1931) and *The Mummy* (1932). Universal was responsible for *Jaws* (1975) and *ET – The Extra Terrestrial* (1982). Universal also operates theme parks in Hollywood, Florida, Japan and Spain.

ALL EIGHTS

Eight eights

Jennifer Eight (1992) • *8 Mile* (2002)
8 MM (1999) • *8 1/2 (1963)*
8 Heads In A Duffel Bag (1997) • *Dinner at Eight* (1933)
Eight Legged Freaks (2002)
Friday the 13th Part VIII: Jason Takes Manhattan (1989)

The eight women of *8 Women* (2002)

Danielle Darrieux – *Mamy*
Catherine Deneuve – *Gaby*
Isabelle Huppert – *Augustine*
Emmanuelle Béart – *Louise*
Fanny Ardant – *Pierrette*
Virginie Ledoyen – *Suzon*
Ludivine Sagnier – *Catherine*
Firmine Richard – *Madame Chanel*

The Crazy Eighty-Eights are the personal protection squad of O Ren Ishii in *Kill Bill: Vol. 1* (2003). The band at the club where The Bride and O Ren fight are called the 5, 6, 7, 8s.

The eponymous bond girl of *Octopussy* (1983) was Swedish former model Maud Adams. Octopussy's diamond-smuggling operations were covered by a circus of deadly female acrobats.

Eight roles of Alec Guinness in *Kind Heart and Coronets* (1949)

The Duke • The Banker
The Parson • The General
Young Ascoyne • Young Henry
Lady Agatha • The Admiral

The eight rules of *Fight Club* (1999)

1. The first rule of Fight Club is: you do not talk about Fight Club.
2. The second rule of Fight Club is: you DO NOT talk about Fight Club.
3. Third rule of Fight Club: someone yells 'Stop!', goes limp, taps out, the fight is over.
4. Fourth rule: only two guys to a fight.
5. Fifth rule: one fight at a time, fellas.
6. Sixth rule: no shirt, no shoes.
7. Seventh rule: fights will go on as long as they have to.
8. And the eighth and final rule: if this is your first night at Fight Club, you have to fight.

ONCE THE MOVIE WAS OVER...

Chitty Chitty Bang Bang turned out not to be so friendly after all.

TAGLINE TEASERS

On which movie posters would you see these taglines?

1. A new comedy about sex, murder and seafood.

2. The first casualty of war is innocence.

Answers on page 153.

TOP 10 MOST SUCCESSFUL FILM SERIES

Series	No. of Films	Years	Total World Gross ($)
James Bond	20	1963–2002	3,630,559,554
Star Wars	5	1977–2002	3,471,554,580
Jurassic Park	3	1993–2001	1,901,027,106
Harry Potter	2	2001–2002	1,832,722,908
The Lord of the Rings	2	2001–2002	1,742,399,971
Batman	4	1989–1997	1,268,376,929
Indiana Jones	3	1981–1989	1,211,716,531
Star Trek	10	1979–2002	1,053,666,245
Men In Black	2	1997–2002	1,013,409,342
Mission: Impossible	2	1996–2000	1,012,391,875

Average time in seconds between each kiss that John Barrymore 53 gives to ladies in Don Juan *(1926)*

THEY SHOULD HAVE STAYED AT HOME

Lee Harvey Oswald (1939–1963)

Oswald was working at the Texas School Book Depository when President Kennedy's motorcade drove past and JFK was shot dead. Although Oswald was convicted of the crime, many believe he could not have fired the fatal shot. He was arrested later that afternoon in the Texas Theatre cinema where he was watching *Cry of Battle* (1963), which was showing as a double bill with *War is Hell* (1963). He was charged with the murder of the President and another police officer. Two days later, while being transfered from the police station to the county jail, he was shot dead, live on television, by local night-club owner Jack Ruby. Ruby claimed he was avenging Jacqueline Kennedy.

QUOTE UNQUOTE

This film cost $31 million.
With that kind of money I could have invaded some country.
Clint Eastwood, US film actor and director

REASONS TO READ THE CREDITS

The credits of *This is Spinal Tap* (1984) say that the band isn't real and adds, 'And there's no Easter Bunny, either!'

'Extra Special Thanks (with cream on top)', 'Special Thanks (no cream, cherries optional)', 'Quite Special Thanks (hold the sweetener)', 'Best Naughty Boy' and 'This line available... Your name here' all roll in the credits of *The Adventures of Priscilla, Queen of the Desert* (1994)

'Gripology... Pete Papanicko-las', 'Generally in charge of a lot of things... Mike Finnell', 'Foreez ... A Jolly Good Fellow', 'Horse... Windy', 'This motion picture is protected under the laws of the United States and other countries. Unauthorized duplication, distribution, or exhibition may result in civil liability or criminal prosecution. So there.', 'Author of *A Tale of Two Cities*... Charles Dickens' and 'Worst Boy... Adolf Hitler' can all be seen at the end of *Airplane!* (1980).

On the soundtrack list to *Hot Shots! Part Deux* (1993), there is a song entitled 'I got a lot of hair for a bald guy and if I wear it like this you won't notice' by Michael Bolton. It also ends with 'Answer to tonight's scrambled movie title: "T-2"' and a pop quiz, which includes such questions as: 'Who was the Art Director?', 'What does Don Miloyevich do?' and 'What character said 'You yankin' my crank?'

MARVELLOUS MONIKERS

Actor WC Fields' has enjoyed some of the daftest character names in film history:

- Egbert Sousé in *The Bank Dick* (*The Bank Detective* in the UK, 1940)
- Cuthbert J Twillie in *My Little Chickadee* (1940)
- Larson E Whipsnade in *You Can't Cheat an Honest Man* (1939)
- T Frothingill Bellows in *The Big Broadcast of 1938* (1938)
- Professor Eustace P McGargle in *Poppy* (1936)
- Ambrose Wolfinger in *Man on the Flying Trapeze* (*The Memory Expert* in the UK, 1935)
- Mr C Ellsworth Stubbins in *Mrs Wiggs of the Cabbage Patch* (1934)
- Nuggetville Sheriff 'Honest John' Hoxley in *Six of a Kind* (1934)
- Augustus Q Winterbottom in *Tillie and Gus* (1933)
- Rollo La Rue in *If I Had a Million* (1932)
- J Effingham Bellweather in *The Golf Specialist* (1930)
- Gabby Gilfoil in *Two Flaming Youths* (1927)
- Elmer Prettywillie in *It's the Old Army Game* (1926)

FORBIDDEN FILMS

No one knows for sure why director Stanley Kubrick voluntarily withdrew his film **A Clockwork Orange** (1971) from the UK, although there are plenty of stories to choose from. Some suggest that the police asked him to do so after several copycat crimes; in one instance a 17-year-old Dutch girl was raped in Lancashire by a gang chanting *Singin' in the Rain*, and in another, a child was beaten by a 16-year-old boy wearing the protagonist Alex's uniform of white overalls, black bowler hat and combat boots, both of which imitated scenes in the film. According to Kubrick's wife, Christiane, the family received several death threats because of the film. Kubrick asked that the film be released only after his death, which was after he died in his sleep on 7 March 1999 of a heart attack.

AVERAGE NUMBER OF FILMS
SEEN PER INHABITANT

Film watching in large, medium and small film-producing countries

Country	1975	1985	1995
USA	5.7	4.4	4.6
Egypt	1.7	1.2	0.2
Cuba	3.6	7.6	2.2

In *The Meaning of Liff* and *The Deeper Meaning of Liff*, Douglas Adams and John Lloyd addressed the English problem in which many everyday occurrences, feelings, objects and people have no words to describe them. By harnessing place names that described these things perfectly but were not really doing very much else, they created a dictionary of comic genius. Here are their thoughts on all things film:

Blean *(n.)* Scientific measure of luminosity; 1 glimmer = 100,000 bleans. Usherettes' torchs are designed to produce between 2.5 and 4 bleans, enabling them to assist you in falling downstairs, treading on people or putting your hand into a Neopolitan tub when reaching for change.

Damnaglaur *(n.)* A certain facial expression which actors are required to demonstrate their mastery of before they are allowed to play *Macbeth*.

Epsworth *(n.)* It is a little-known fact that an earlier draft of the final line of the film *Gone with the Wind* had Clark Gable saying 'Frankly my dear I don't give an epsworth', the line being eventually changed on the grounds that it might not be understood in Iowa, or indeed anywhere.

Gonnabarn *(n.)* An afternoon wasted on watching an old movie on TV.

Imber *(vb)* To lean from side to side while watching a car chase in the cinema.

Lowther *(vb.)* (Of a large group of people who have been to the cinema together.) To stand aimlessly about on the pavement and argue about whether to go and eat a Chinese meal nearby or an Indian meal at a restaurant which somebody says is very good but isn't certain where it is, or just go home, or have a Chinese meal nearby – until by the time agreement is reached everything is shut.

Ossining *(ptcpl.vb)* Trying to see past the person sitting in front of you at the cinema.

Pantperthog *(n.)* An actor whose only talent is to stay fat.

Papworth Everard *(n.)* Technical term for the fifth take of an orgasm scene during the making of a pornographic film.

Rochester *(n.)* One who is able to gain occupation of the armrests on both sides of their cinema or aircraft seat.

Spiddle *(vb.)* To fritter away a perfectly good life pretending to develop film projects.

Yonder Bognie *(n.)* The kind of restaurant advertised as 'just three minutes from this cinema' which clearly nobody ever goes to and, even if they had ever contemplated it, have certainly changed their minds since seeing the advert.

TOP 20 MEN'S FILMS

Star Wars (1977)
The Great Escape (1963)
The Godfather (1972)
Scarface (1983)
Pulp Fiction (1994)
The Sting (1973)
Apocalypse Now (1979)
Goodfellas (1990)
Bullitt (1968)
Reservoir Dogs (1992)
Full Metal Jacket (1987)
The Shawshank Redemption (1994)
The Matrix (1999)
Dumb and Dumber (1994)
Lock, Stock and Two Smoking Barrels (1998)
Taxi Driver (1976)
Raging Bull (1980)
Blade Runner (1982)
The Lord of the Rings: The Fellowship of the Ring (2001)
Wayne's World (1992)

According to the 14,000 people who answered a 2004 UK
supermarket online survey.

POPPING TO THE MOVIES

It is thought that the first corn was popped some 5,000 years ago by the Native American Indians. Popcorn was used as a dish as well as a decoration in religious ceremonies. Columbus and his men purchased popcorn necklaces from the natives in the West Indies.

Although popcorn was a novelty for the European conquerors of the New World, it wasn't until the Depression years that this cheap food was appreciated for its ability to stretch the family budget. By 1947, 85% of US cinemas sold the white fluffy morsels in their lobbies and a poll from the 1950s showed that two out of three television watchers ate popcorn as often as four nights a week. The popcorn bucket has since become a symbol of the movie industry and the trophy for the MTV Movie Awards.

Popcorn derives its name from the Middle English word 'poppe', meaning 'explosive sound.' For popcorn to pop, a kernel needs to have a water content of at least 14% so that under heat, the water expands to steam and the nugget explodes into the puffy cinema snack. Unpopped kernels are called duds.

A STRANGE WAY TO GO

Michael Findlay, horror film director of *Snuff* (1976), was decapitated by a helicopter blade in 1977.

Tennessee Williams, playwright and screenwriter, choked to death on a plastic bottle cap in 1983.

Bob Crane, actor in *Superdad* (1974), was found murdered in a hotel room in 1978. His death is still unsolved.

Isadora Duncan, actress and dancer, died in 1927 of accidental strangulation when her scarf caught in her car wheel, throwing her forcibly from the vehicle and strangling her.

Dominique Dunne, actress in *Poltergeist* (1982), was choked by her boyfriend, John Sweeny, after she ended their abusive relationship in 1982. She was rendered brain dead and was removed from her life support five days later.

Sharon Tate, actress, was stabbed to death in 1969 by the Manson 'family'. She was eight and a half months pregnant with Roman Polanski's son at the time.

MIXED-UP MOVIESTARS

Unscramble these famous actors
A WILD OLD MENACE • OLD WEST ACTION
HE'S GROWN LAZY AND CRAZED
Answer on page 153.

WORDS ON FILM

In the 1930s you learnt how to behave as a human being from movies. You learnt how to smoke, how to hold a cigarette. I wanted to become a reporter because I lusted after a belted trenchcoat like the one Joel McCrea wore in Hitchcock's *Foreign Correspondence*. Girls kissed with their eyes closed and raising themselves up on tiptoe, because that was the cute shot in American movies. We believed in Hollywood. Cinemas themselves were special. Nobody had central heating, so it was warm. It was dark: 'six penn'orth of dark' was what people were after. The cinema was our motel. And it was opulent in the way nothing else in your life was. They were called 'picture palaces' for a very good reason. At the Empire, Leicester Square, the toilets were truly lavish: 'I dreamt I dwelt in marble halls' had real meaning. Before the cinema opened the men on the staff were given cigars to puff, so that when you came into the foyer it had that smell of luxury.

Denis Norden in *Seeing in the Dark:*
A Compendium of Cinemagoing

BEFORE THEY WERE FAMOUS

Kathy Bates, *cashier in the gift shop in
New York's Museum of Modern Art*
Warren Beatty, *cocktail bar pianist*
Pierce Brosnan, *mini cab driver*
Gabriel Byrne, *plumber*
James Caan, *rodeo rider*
Willem Dafoe, *magazine binder at* Penthouse
Danny de Vito, *janitor*
Tom Hanks, *bellhop*
Rutger Hauer, *electrician*
Bob Hoskins, *nightclub bouncer*
Michael Keaton, *cab driver*
Ben Kingsley, *penicillin tester*
Walter Matthau, *filing clerk*
Paul Newman, *encyclopedia salesman*
Robert Redford, *pavement artist*
Mickey Rourke, *pretzel seller*
Rene Russo, *eye glass factory worker*
Kate Winslet, *shop assistant in a delicatessen*
Edward Woodward, *trainee sanitary engineer*

QUOTE UNQUOTE

*Here I am paying big money to you writers and what for?
All you do is change the words.*
Samuel Goldwyn, film producer

MOVIE URBAN LEGENDS

Marisa Tomei

Legend: Marisa Tomei won the Academy Award for best supporting actress in 1992 for *My Cousin Vinnie* because Oscar-presenter Jack Palance read the wrong name by mistake.

This is not true despite the persistent rumours that sprung up soon after the ceremony in 1993. The rumour was that Vanessa Redgrave was the 'real' winner of the award, for *Howard's End*. The reason behind this mix-up was supposedly either a planned subterfuge on the part of Palance or that he was mistaken through personal error, drunkenness or an inability to read the name on the card. However, the story has been officially denied, since at the Oscars, the regulators of the awards, PricewaterhouseCoopers have representatives stationed at the side of the stage in case an incorrect name is read out. If that does happen, one of the officials immediately steps out and announces the real winner.

*Number of takes it took Marilyn Monroe to say 'Where's the Bourbon?' 59
correctly in* Some Like it Hot *(1959)*

Usher

You are responsible for the cinema audience being safely and properly seated. You also examine tickets as people enter the cinema, deal with any arguments over seating and disturbances during the film.

Good Points
• See films for free
• Flexible hours
• No formal qualifications needed

Bad Points
• You have to see the same films again and again
• You may have to work very late shifts and weekends
• You have to be polite to children who throw popcorn in your face

Projectionist

You operate the projectors that show the films in cinemas. You also receive the film from the distributor and maintain them, repairing them when necessary. You ensure that the film runs smoothly during a showing by loading the spools and splicing lengths of film together if there are any breaks.

Good Points
• You get to watch films all day
• No formal training or qualifications are needed

Bad Points
• You would have to watch the same films for weeks on end
• You will probably spend most of your time in small windowless rooms

Film Reviewer

•You watch new films that are about to be released and write a review of the film for publication to inform the audience of your opinion so they can determine if they want to see the film themselves.

Good Points
• You can say what you want about the films you see
• You may get the opportunity to meet film stars
• Flexible hours

Bad Points
• You have to watch the terrible films, as well as the good ones
• Numb bum

Unemployment

You do… nothing.

Good Points
• You can see films whenever you want
• You can go to afternoon showings and have the whole cinema to yourself
• Matinee cheap rates

Bad Points
• It doesn't pay
• It's a bit lonely
• You realise you are that weirdo who is always in the cinema on their own

Mr and Mrs Jones were beginning to regret sending their daughter to Hogwarts.

THE KID STAYS IN THE PICTURE

Shirley Temple (1928–)

'I stopped believing in Santa Claus when my mother took me to see him in a department store, and he asked for my autograph.'

Bouncy, curly-haired Shirley shot to super stardom during the Depression years in America. Her cheerful film appearances won over a huge fan base and she was the biggest star in Hollywood in 1936, 1937 and 1938. She has not appeared in any films since 1949 but has been a US ambassador and UN delegate for many years.

During the 1970s a genre of films known as 'blaxploitation' depicted stereotypes of African-Americans and were written and directed by white men. To the surprise of many, the films were widely popular with black audiences and were the first films to portray black actors in major roles. However, not everyone approved; The Coalition Against Blaxploitation was formed in reaction to the films and received wide media attention.

The first blaxploitation film was *Sweet Sweetback's Baadasssss Song* (1971). At the time no Hollywood studio would finance the film because it had an all-black cast and so Melvin Van Peebles, the director, writer and actor of the film, financed it himself. The film became a huge hit and made $10 million.

I'm Gonna Git You Sucka (1988) is a spoof of the blaxploitation genre and starred many of the stars of the original films of the 1970s. Some of these stars have enjoyed a revival in recent years. Isaac Hayes who starred in *Truck Turner* (1974) and wrote the Oscar-winning score for *Shaft* (1971) features in the television show *South Park* as Chef. The part was supposed to be a one-off but audiences reacted so well to the part that he became a regular character. Pam Grier, who starred in *Foxy Brown* (1974) and many more blaxploitation films in the 1970s, enjoyed a return to top billing in Quentin Tarantino's *Jackie Brown* (1997).

10 FUNNIEST FILMS

1.	*Some Like It Hot*	(1959)
2.	*Tootsie*	(1982)
3.	*Dr Strangelove or: How I Learned to Stop Worrying and Love the Bomb*	(1964)
4.	*Annie Hall*	(1977)
5.	*Duck Soup*	(1933)
6.	*Blazing Saddles*	(1974)
7.	*M*A*S*H*	(1970)
8.	*It Happened One Night*	(1934)
9.	*The Graduate*	(1967)
10.	*Airplane!*	(1980)

As selected in a poll conducted by The American Film Institute in 2000. The 500 nominated films were judged by a jury of 1,800 leaders from the film community, including directors, screenwriters, actors, editors, cinematographers, critics, historians and film executives.

BRITAIN'S DEADLIEST WEAPON

In the first 20 James Bond movies:

Sean Connery starred in seven Bond movies
George Lazenby in one
Roger Moore in seven
Timothy Dalton in two
Pierce Brosnan in four

- Bond has 18 martinis, five of which he orders himself, two of which he never receives. The rest are prepared and brought to him.

- In his seven appearances as Bond, Sean Connery utters the phrase 'shaken, not stirred' only once, in *Goldfinger*.

- Bond is told 33 times that he will die, and he makes love 79 times. Of the 58 Bond girls, 29 were brunettes, 25 blondes, and 4 redheads. Women moaned 'Oh, James!' 16 times.

Places where James Bond made love:

Hotel room (19 times), London flat (2), at her place (15), someone else's place (2), on a train (3), in a barn (2), in a forest (2), in a gypsy tent (2), hospital (2), in a plane (2), in a submarine (1), in a car (1), on a motorised iceberg (1), in, around, under, or by water (25 times).

WORDS ON FILM

JC: Bogart could be a little argumentative when he had had something to drink, and on *The Treasure of the Sierra Madre* (1948), which Huston also made with him, they had a big argument and Bogey started swinging at John. John was very tall and had a tremendous reach so he just reached out and grasped Bogey's nose and left him there thrashing about until he had cooled off.

JB: Katharine Hepburn proved herself to be pretty tough on the film.

JC: We all had this terrible sickness and Kate was as sick as the rest of us. Of course, Bogey and Huston were never ill, and the joke is, it was because they only ever drank whiskey and never touched the water. The rest of the unit were very ill and so was Kate, but she was very brave to go in front of the camera and act like that, because her face was often white or sickly green. She sometimes had a bucket just out of camera range, which she would throw up into between takes.

Of course, at the time, we didn't know it was the water making us sick, but the irony was that it was known that Kate was using bottled Evian water to wash her hair, which was considered very wasteful. If only she had drunk it instead of washing in it, she would have been fine.

Justin Bowyer, *Conversations With Jack Cardiff, Art, light and direction in cinema*, discussing the filming of *The African Queen*

A WEEK AT THE MOVIES

First Monday in October (1981)
Stormy Monday (1988)

Black Tuesday (1954)
If It's Tuesday This Must Be Belgium (1969)
Never on Tuesday (1988)

Ash Wednesday (1973)
Any Wednesday (1966)

Thursday's Game (1974)
Great Scout and Cathouse Thursday (1976)
Thursday (1998)

His Girl Friday (1940)
Freaky Friday (1976) and (2003)
Thank God It's Friday (1978)
Friday The 13th (1980)

Saturday Night Fever (1977)
Mr Saturday Night (1992)

In New York Sunday (1963)
Sunday Bloody Sunday (1971)
Six Ways To Sunday (1997)
Any Given Sunday (1999)

QUOTE UNQUOTE

When I see those ads with the quote 'you'll have to see this picture twice', I know it's the kind of picture I don't want to see once.
Pauline Kael, US film reviewer

THE CRITICAL LIST

Harry Knowles (1971–)

Intrinsically linked with his film review website 'Ain't it Cool' (www.aintitcool.com), Harry Knowles is an online film reviewer who embraces the geekier side of film, especially the blockbuster, superhero and comic book genres. The super-sized (he reportedly weighs more than 20 stone) redheaded film fan started his website in 1996 from his hometown of Austin, Texas. The philosophy behind his reviews is that 'film review[ing] doesn't begin and end with the opening and ending titles. There is more to it. What we do and who we are affects the review. Instead of hiding that, I share it. You should know who your reviewer is, what he was anticipating and what happened to him/her on that particular day.'

64 *Year, in the twentieth century, when films shown in Malta were first allowed to show two-piece bathing suits*

FILM STAR NICKNAMES

The Look	Lauren Bacall
The 'It' Girl	Clara Bow
America's Sweetheart	Mary Pickford
The Muscles From Brussels	Jean-Claude Van Damme
The Duke	John Wayne
The Great Profile	John Barrymore
The King	Clark Gable
The Platinum Blonde	Jean Harlow
Million Dollar Legs	Betty Grable
The Sweater Girl	Lana Turner
Sly/The Italian Stallion	Sylvester Stallone

A ROARING SUCCESS

When Samuel Goldwyn founded his film production company in 1916, he asked Howard Dietz, a young advertising executive recently graduated from Columbia University to design a logo that was 'big and loud enough to be heard even from the silent screen.' Dietz was inspired by his university's mascot and its fight song, 'Roar, Lion, Roar', to create the logo that was to become the trademark of the merged Metro, Goldwyn and Meyer studios (MGM) in 1924. Several trained lions have posed as Leo the Lion. Slats, the first lion posing for the Goldwyn trademark, was followed by Jackie after the formation of MGM. Tanner was the first MGM lion of the Technicolor era. For many years Jackie and Tanner shared the role of Leo the Lion. In 1986 as MGM shifted its focus from films to hotels, the legendary MGM logo was removed from the top of its old main studio building in Culver City, thus putting a symbolic end to the famous roaring lion of the film industry.

CUT TO THE CHASE

Unlike today when film budgets can allow for million dollar chases to happen before the opening credits have even begun, many early films ended in chase sequences that were seen as the climax of the whole film experience. To add some kind of length and depth to the film, the chases were preceded by obligatory, and sometimes dull, storylines.

The literal use of cut to the chase as a director's instruction can be traced to the 1920s, specifically JP McEvoy's 1929 novel *Hollywood Girl*. It has the script direction: 'Jannings escapes... cut to chase.' However, it wasn't until the early 1980s that the phrase became familiar in everyday conversation.

Number of years between the first feature-length animation to win an Oscar 65
and the introduction of the Animated Feature Film Oscar in 2000

The infamous shower scene in *Psycho* (1960) was shot in December 1959.

To get a satisfactory sound for the stabbing scene, Hitchcock experimented with several fruits until he decided upon a Turkish melon. For the blood, Hitchcock used chocolate sauce, a popular technique with directors of black and white films.

Some people have said that Hitchcock engineered the water to suddenly become ice cold when Janet Leigh was attacked, but this has never been corroborated.

Hitchcock used Janet Leigh in the shower for shots of her face, hands and midriff but the rest of the shots were of a nude model called Marli Renfro.

Once the film was released, it generated an enormous amount of hype, thanks in no small part to Hitchcock's masterful marketing. Hitchcock prepared a booklet for cinema managers called 'The Care and Handling of *Pyscho*'. He also issued clocks for cinemas to remind audiences when the film started and a notice that stated that the cinema manager, at the risk of his life, would not allow anyone into the film once it had started. Cinema managers were also forbidden to follow the film by a short film or a newsreel and the lights in the cinema were to be left down for at least 30 seconds so that 'the suspense of *Psycho* [could be] indelibly engraved in the minds of the audience.'

Hitchcock also received a letter from an angry father whose daughter refused to have a bath after seeing *Les Diaboliques* (1954) and now refused to have a shower. Ever the diplomat, Hitchcock sent a note back saying 'Send her to the dry cleaners.'

BIG SCREEN BEASTIES

Name: Pal

Breed: Rough collie

Film: *Lassie Come Home* (1943)

Trivia: In his first film role in *Lassie Come Home*, Pal earned a salary of $250 per week. A young Elizabeth Taylor also made an appearance in the film as Priscilla. However, although she was to become the first actress to earn $1 million for one film, on this film she took home less than the dog; a mere $100 a week.

Pal went on to star in a further six films that earned millions for MGM and more than $200,000 for his own doggie biscuit fund.

In 1975 *Esquire* magazine added Lassie to its list of 'Great American Things.'

VAMPING IT UP

Famous screen vampies

Max Schreck in *Nosferatu: A Symphony of Horror* (1922)
Bela Lugosi in *Dracula* (1931)
Christopher Lee in *The Horror of Dracula* (1958)
George Hamilton in *Love at First Bite* (1979)
Catherine Deneuve in *The Hunger* (1980)
Lauren Hutton in *Once Bitten* (1985)
Kiefer Sutherland in *The Lost Boys* (1987)
Nicolas Cage in *Vampire's Kiss* (1989)
Gary Oldman in *Bram Stoker's Dracula* (1992)
Paul Reubens in *Buffy the Vampire Slayer* (1992)
Tom Cruise, Brad Pitt and Kirsten Dunst in *Interview with a Vampire: The Vampire Chronicles* (1994)
Willem Dafoe in *Shadow of the Vampire* (2000)

RE-PLAYING FIELDS

The wisdom of actor WC Fields (1880–1946)

- 'Twas a woman drove me to drink. I never had the courtesy to thank her.'

- 'Hey, who took the cork off my lunch?'

- 'Start every day with a smile, and get it over with.'

- 'What fiend put pineapple juice in my pineapple juice?'

- 'If at first you don't succeed, try, try again. Then give up. No use being a damned fool about it.'

- 'Once ...in the wilds of Afghanistan, I lost my corkscrew, and we were forced to live on nothing but food and water for days.'

- 'I am free of all prejudice. I hate everyone equally.'

- 'I feel like a midget with muddy feet has been walking over my tongue all night.'

- 'I exercise extreme self-control. I never drink anything stronger than gin before breakfast.'

- 'Everyone must believe in something. I believe I'll have another drink.'

- 'Few things in life are more embarrassing than the necessity of having to inform an old friend that you have just got engaged to his fiancée.'

- 'Madam, there's no such thing as a tough child – if you parboil them first for seven hours, they always come out tender.'

TAGLINE TEASERS

On which movie posters would you see these taglines?

1. To enter the mind of a killer she must challenge the mind of a madman.

2. Can two friends sleep together and still love each other in the morning?

Answers on page 153.

AND WHO ARE YOU?

Characters without a name:

Marilyn Monroe in *The Seven Year Itch* (1955)… The Girl
Paul McGann in *Withnail and I* (1987)… I
Edward Norton in *Fight Club* (1999)… Narrator
Uma Thurman in *Kill Bill Vol. 1* (2003)… The Bride
Joan Fontaine in *Rebecca* (1940)… The second Mrs de Winter
Crispin Glover in *Charlie's Angels* (2000)… Thin Man
William B Davis in *The X-Files* (1998)… Cigarette Smoking Man
Kevin Costner in *The Postman* (1997)… The Postman
Wiley Wiggins in *Waking Life* (2001)… Main Character
Clint Eastwood in *The Good, the Bad and the Ugly* (1966)… The Man With No Name

WORDS ON FILM

And this leads to another important difference between American movies and my movies. As I mentioned earlier, the action scenes in American films are pretty much scripted out every step of the way. Every punch and kick and tumble has to be storyboarded in advance, because the stuntmen or special effects people have to be prepared for what's going to happen.

In the scripts for my films, the fights are barely described – it's just, 'Jackie fights the henchman as they climb up the scaffolding.' How the fight goes is completely up in the air, because it's all decided right before the cameras roll. I think of different props I want to use, and my stuntmen suggest different fighting stunts to incorporate. We'll stand and brainstorm around the location, trying out different techniques. It's slow work, maybe, but the results are worth it – every screen fight that I've ever shot is completely integrated with the scenery, the props, and even the bystanders. It's like jazz: I never know what's gong to come out until the mood and the environment come together.

Jackie Chan, *I am Jackie Chan, My Life in Action*

68 *Year, in the twentieth century, when the f-word was first said in a film (*I'll Never Forget What's 'Isname*)*

SOME FILM FIRSTS

First feature film ever made: *The Story of the Kelly Gang* (1906).

First British feature film: *Oliver Twist* (1912).

First film shown to a paying audience: *Young Griffo v Battling Charles Barnett* (New York, 20 May 1895).

First film festival: The Venice Film Festival at Hotel Excelsior (1932).

First film to end on a freeze frame: *La Roue* (1923) The writer and director Abel Gance came up with the idea for this film the day his wife was diagnosed with tuberculosis and finished it the day she died.

First in-flight movie: Conan Doyle's *The Lost World* (1925). It was shown on an Imperial Airways flight in a converted Handley-Page bomber from London to Paris, in April 1925.

First Hollywood film studio: Centaur Film Company.

First song composed for a film: *Mother I Still Have You.* The song was composed for the first 'talkie' *The Jazz Singer* in 1927. It was sung by Al Jolson.

First Oscar won by a Brit: Charles Laughton for *Private Life of Henry VIII* (1933).

First film star on a postage stamp: Grace Kelly and her husband Prince Rainier III of Monaco on a stamp in April 1956 to commemorate their wedding.

First shot from a helicopter: *They Live By Night* (1949) The UK title was *The Twisted Road*.

First British 'talkie': *Blackmail* (1929) directed by Alfred Hitchcock.

First remake: *The Great Train Robbery* (1904) was a remake of the film of the same name from 1903.

First multiplex in Britain: The Point in Milton Keynes in 1985.

LOOPY LANGUAGES

Sebastiane (1976) was the first film to feature dialogue entirely in Latin. For added realism the script was given to a classics scholar who acted as translator. He went to great efforts to convey the erotic script into vulgar Latin of the third century. The film is also the only English film ever to be released in Britain with English subtitles.

Incubus (1965) is the only film to have been made using only Esperanto. The choice of Esperanto was supposedly made to give the film an air of the supernatural.

25 years of the top-grossing films at the box office

1975 *Jaws*

1976 *Rocky*

1977 *Star Wars*

1978 *Grease*

1979 *Kramer vs. Kramer*

1980 *Star Wars: Episode V – The Empire Strikes Back*

1981 *Raiders of the Lost Ark*

1982 *ET – The Extra Terrestrial*

1983 *Star Wars: Episode VI – Return of the Jedi*

1984 *Ghostbusters*

1985 *Back to the Future*

1986 *Top Gun*

1987 *Three Men and a Baby*

1988 *Rain Man*

1989 *Batman*

1990 *Home Alone*

1991 *Terminator 2: Judgement Day*

1992 *Aladdin*

1993 *Jurassic Park*

1994 *Forrest Gump*

1995 *Toy Story*

1996 *Independence Day*

1997 *Titanic*

1998 *Saving Private Ryan*

1999 *Star Wars: Episode I – The Phantom Menace*

2000 *How the Grinch Stole Christmas*

QUOTE UNQUOTE

Of all the creatures on the planet, man is the only one who derives immense pleasure from watching a movie that cost $90m to make drop dead at the box office.
Joe Queenan, US writer and film reviewer

MOVIE URBAN LEGENDS

Brandon Lee

Legend: The scene in which Brandon Lee was fatally wounded was left in the final cut of *The Crow* (1994).

Brandon Lee died at the age of 28 while filming *The Crow*. His death was a tragic accident resulting from a faulty prop. Rumours sprung up probably because of the mysterious death of his father, Bruce Lee who died aged 32 of a brain oedema (swelling) under what have been described as extraordinary circumstances. In the *The Crow*, Brandon Lee was shot at with a blank from a gun in a scene where he enters his apartment carrying his groceries and is killed by street thugs. A blank was fired but there was also a fragment of a dummy bullet in the barrel from an earlier shot. When the gun was fired, the fragment hit Lee in the side and fatally wounded him. The death was found to be accidental. The film was completed using digital tricks and scenes with a double. Nowhere in the film is there a scene with Lee entering an apartment with a bag of groceries.

70 *Number of years that a film is protected by copyright after all the principle film makers have died*

THE SHORT VERSION

Shortest ever film titles

It (1927)
The film gave its star Clara Bow the nickname of the 'It' girl.

M (1931 and remake in 1951)
The film's title was originally 'The Murderers are Among Us,' a thinly-veiled reference to the Nazi Party's group of street thugs, the 'SA'. The change to 'M' was prompted by director Fritz Lang's fear that they would realise it was a reference to them.

X (1963)

If.... (1968)
Set in director Lindsay Anderson's old school, the film was a strong condemnation of the public school system. However, to get permission to shoot in the school Anderson knew he could not show the script to the staff and so wrote a fake script and gave it an unthreatening title. The producer's secretary suggested taking 'If' from the Rudyard Kipling poem. Anderson added the four dots later.

Z (1969)

W (1974)
Also known as: *I Want Her Dead* (1974).

I.Q. (1994)

Da (1988)
A shortening of 'dad'.

FM (1978)
Many AM radio stations played an edited version of the movie's title song in which an over-dubbed 'A' was substituted for the 'F' of FM.

10 (1979)
Widely understood to refer to Bo Derek's looks, the rating actually given to her character's looks in the scene where the subject arises is 11 out of 10.

Q (1981)
The title 'Q' is short for Quetzlcoatl, the Aztec god who was half reptile and half bird.

F/X (1986)

Pi (1998)

K2 (1992)

Ed (1996)
The title refers to a monkey that Matt Le Blanc has to bond with.

Go (1999)

O (2001)
An update of *Othello*, set in an American high school.

CQ (2001)
'CQ' is the Morse code phrase for 'seek you' (a call for contact).

X2 (2003)
The sequel to *X-Men* (2000)

Number of songs in the Indian musical Indra Sabha *(1932),* 71 *the most in any film*

Go ahead, take my sleigh.

WHO HAS THE MOST CINEMAS?

Curious to compare... a random selection of countries and the number of cinemas they have.

Country	Number of cinemas in 1995
Argentina	427
Australia	1,137
Belarus	3,780
Bolivia	30
Denmark	165
France	4,365
India	21,848 (in 1996)
Italy	3,816
Japan	1,776
New Zealand	255
Spain	2,090
Suriname	1 (in 1996)
UK	2,019
USA	29,731

72 *Year, in the twentieth century, with the highest worldwide output of horror films (189)*

WORDS ON FILM

Filming *Superman* was sometimes tedious and exasperating, I spent months hanging on wires for brief moments in the movie that would then have to be reshot. But ultimately it was a wonderful experience. One of my favourite memories is of running into John Gielgud in a hallway at Pinewood Studios. We had met at a social occasion; now I was dressed in full Superman regalia. As he shook my hand he said, 'So delightful to see you. What are you doing now?'

Christopher Reeve, *Still Me*

NOT A CHEAP-A-SAURUS

With budgets that match the GNP of small nations, Hollywood films are not known for scrimping and saving. Keen to make their money back, producers are more than happy to spend on promotion too. However the record for money spent on a film's promotion goes to *Jurassic Park* (1993). Universal Pictures and licensed merchandisers spent $68 million promoting the Spielberg film in the US alone. This was at least $5 million more than the film cost to make.

HOLLYWOOD SIGNS

The star-studded sign of Hollywood first arrived in Tinsel Town in 1923 and still stands on top of Mount Lee. At the time it read 'Hollywoodland' ('land' was removed in 1945) and was an advertisement for a real estate company. The sign cost a whopping $21,000 and required 4,000 20-watt light bulbs. Each of the letters is 30 feet wide and 50 feet tall, and are made up of 3 x 9 metal squares. Hollywood fell in love with its sign and in 1973, it was classified as an official historic monument.

One Welsh actress gave the sign a less glamorous type of notoriety when she threw herself off it in 1932. Peg Entwhistle had made her name on Broadway and set her heart on finding fame on the big screen. However after appearing in only one film she became so demoralised that she climbed up on the sign and threw herself off the letter H.

In 1978, when Pope John Paul II visited, the sign was tampered with to read 'Holywood'. In 1987, the sign was altered to read 'Ollywood' in reference to the scandal surrounding the sale of arms by Ronald Reagan's government to Iran though the intermediary Oliver North. And finally, in 1976, the sign was changed to read 'Hollyweed' as a celebration of the relaxed marijuana laws.

COMING SOON

Most moviegoers are familiar with Don LaFontaine, even though they have no idea who he is. For the last 40 years his unmistakably deep voice has been used on over 4,000 trailers, including *2001: A Space Odyssey* (1968), *M*A*S*H* (1970), *The Untouchables* (1987), *Ghostbusters* (1984), *Field of Dreams* (1989) *Terminator 2: Judgement Day* (1991) and *Batman* (1989). His first trailer was for the *Gunfighters at Casa Grande* (1964): 'In a blur of speed, their hands flashed down to their holsters and came up spitting fire.' LaFontaine wrote the line himself and spent the next decades writing and recording voiceovers until he became the first person directors called when making a trailer. He records about 15 voiceovers every day and reportedly earns a six- or seven-figure salary.

TEN GREATEST MOVIE STARS

MEN	WOMEN
1. Humphrey Bogart	1. Katharine Hepburn
2. Cary Grant	2. Bette Davis
3. James Stewart	3. Audrey Hepburn
4. Marlon Brando	4. Ingrid Bergman
5. Fred Astaire	5. Greta Garbo
6. Henry Fonda	6. Marilyn Monroe
7. Clark Gable	7. Elizabeth Taylor
8. James Cagney	8. Judy Garland
9. Spencer Tracy	9. Marlene Dietrich
10. Charlie Chaplin	10. Joan Crawford

In a ballot held by the American Film Institute in 1999, the greatest movie stars were decided using the definition that: 'an "American screen legend" is an actor or a team of actors with a significant screen presence in American feature-length films whose screen debut occurred in or before 1950, or whose screen debut occurred after 1950 but whose death has marked a completed body of work.' The list was selected by leaders from the American film community, including artists, historians, critics and other cultural leaders, who chose from a list of 250 nominees in each gender category, as compiled by AFI historians.

QUOTE UNQUOTE

I never went to a John Wayne movie to find a philosophy to live by or to absorb a profound message. I went for the simple pleasure of spending a couple of hours seeing the bad guys lose.
Mike Royko, US writer and journalist

74 *Number of years after publication of Joseph Conrad's* Heart of Darkness *that Francis Ford Coppola began shooting* Apocalypse Now *(1979).*

*The Americans sent Bruce Willis to prevent Armageddon;
the British sent Major Hobson and his trusty umbrella.*

POWERFUL PIGS

The landmark British animated film *Animal Farm* (1954), based on George Orwell's novel, is said to have been funded and influenced by the CIA. The CIA obtained the film rights to *Animal Farm* from Orwell's widow, Sonia, and supposedly funded the production surreptitiously, giving it an anti-Communist spin. Howard Hunt, best known for his involvement in the Watergate break-in, led the operation. Some sources believe that the ending of the story was altered by the CIA to press home their message. However, others maintain that the discrepancy between the book and the film was merely an artistic decision.

*Average number of films US director DW Griffith made a year 75
between 1908 and 1913*

MIXED-UP MOVIE STARS

Unscramble these famous actors
ERROR ON BIDET • I'M SO CUTER
I, THE LAZY BLOATER
Answers on page 153.

WORDS ON FILM

On an aeroplane you're helpless. The film you see is somebody else's choice, and it usually has George Segal in it. Once I watched a whole movie with the wrong soundtrack. It was Fletch, and when Chevy Chase spoke it was Julie Andrews who came out of his mouth.

You're trapped in your headphones and trapped in your seat. You feel helpless, too, because you're watching it in danger. Cinemas are safe, that is one of their charms. They're dark and upholstered and warm as the womb. There's staff with uniforms to look after you. A plane cabin tries to fool you with the same set-up, but suddenly it meets turbulence, bumps and jolts, and three hundred of you sit there thinking of the drop beneath. In the middle of *A Man For All Seasons* there's a ping, and on come the little red signs: FASTEN YOUR SEATBELT. In front of the celluloid swordfight three hundred souls fear for their lives.

Once, coming back from New York, we were all watching a romantic comedy. It was interrupted by the captain's voice telling us that thanks to the strong following winds we would be arriving in London three quarters of an hour before schedule.

Trouble was, the film wasn't nearly finished. So a stewardess fast forwarded it. We sat, rigid in our seats, as chunks of gabbled plot sped by. Our suave heroes were transformed into Laurel and Hardy: suburban life speeded up into some manic, coronary inducing rush hour. How time flies! We were at our stewardess's mercy. She had promoted herself into the film's second editor, and slowed it down to normal at the bits she liked, and thought we would appreciate. These bits were the love scenes. Suddenly, once they were in each other's arms, our hero and heroine acted like normal human beings. According to our blonde stewardess, herself an object of fantasy, all life was a mindless rush, gabbled nonsense, sweaty commuting between the only moments that made sense, the embrace of a man and a woman. And how beautifully she stage managed it: as we touched down at Heathrow, the final credits were rolling.

Deborah Moggach in *Seeing in the Dark: A Compendium of Cinemagoing*

THEY SHOULD HAVE STAYED AT HOME

John Dillinger (1903–1934)

Dillinger was a high profile US bank robber during the Depression era. As part of a ruthless gang, he robbed banks at a time when people's life savings were being wiped out by the economic crisis and spent many years in prison for his crimes. When Dillinger escaped from prison in March 1934 and continued to rob banks, he was named Public Enemy Number One by the US Justice Department's Division of Investigation (later to become the FBI). A $10,000 reward was offered for his capture. On 22 July 1934, Dillinger went to the cinema and watched *Manhattan Melodrama* (1934), a gangster film starring Clark Gable, William Powell and Myrna Loy at the Biograph Theater in Chicago. He went with his girlfriend Polly Hamilton and Anna Sage (or Ana Campanas – different accounts dispute her name), a brothel owner who was facing deportation charges. However Sage had tipped off the FBI and when the threesome left the cinema the FBI were waiting and opened fire, killing Dillinger.

THE PRICE OF A SEAT

Countries with the most expensive cinema tickets:

		Average ticket ($)
1.	Japan	10.08
2.	Switzerland	8.13
3.	Taiwan	7.84
4.	Iceland	6.99
5.	Sweden	6.86
6.	UK	6.64
7.	Denmark	6.51
8.	Norway	6.14
9.	Finland	5.98
10.	Israel	5.70

THE KID STAYS IN THE PICTURE

Mickey Rooney (1920–)

'I was a 14-year-old boy for 30 years.'

Mickey starred in his first film when he was six. He became a huge child star and starred in 50 silent comedies between 1927 and 1933. By 1939 he earned a rumoured $23,000 for *Babes in Arms*. However he found it hard to make the change over to adult star after he came back from World War Two and although he has appeared in hundreds of films throughout his life, he never eclipsed his early fame.

Percentage of protagonists in the top 250 grossing US films of 2002 who 77
were male

In 1916 the new President of BBFC (British Board of Film Classification, formed in 1912), TP O'Connor, compiled a list of grounds for censorship to try and create an authoritative body of film classification. His suggestions included banning:

1. Indecorous, ambiguous and irreverent titles and subtitles.
2. Cruelty to animals.
3. Drunken scenes carried to excess.
4. Vulgar accessories in the staging.
5. The modus operandi of criminals.
6. Cruelty to young infants and excessive cruelty and torture to adults, especially women.
7. Unnecessary exhibition of under-clothing.
8. The exhibition of profuse bleeding.
9. Nude figures.
10. Offensive vulgarity, and impropriety in conduct and dress.
11. Indecorous dancing.
12. Excessively passionate love scenes.
13. Bathing scenes passing the limits of propriety.
14. References to controversial politics.
15. Relations of capital and labour.
16. Scenes tending to disparage public characters and institutions.
17. Realistic horrors of warfare.
18. Scenes and incidents calculated to afford information to the enemy.
19. Incidents having a tendency to disparage our Allies.
20. Scenes holding up the King's uniform to contempt or ridicule.
21. Subjects dealing with India, in which British Officers are seen in an odious light, and otherwise attempting to suggest the disloyalty of Native States or bringing into disrepute British prestige in the Empire.
22. Gruesome murders and strangulation scenes.
23. Executions.
24. The drug habit eg opium, morphia, cocaine, etc.
25. Subjects dealing with White Slave traffic.
26. Subjects dealing with premeditated seduction of girls.
27. Scenes suggestive of immorality.
28. Indelicate sexual situations.
29. Situations accentuating delicate marital relations.
30. Men and women in bed together.
31. Illicit relationships.
32. Prostitution and procuration.
33. Incidents indicating the actual perpetuation of criminal assaults on women.
34. Scenes depicting the effect of venereal disease – inherited or acquired.
35. Incidents suggestive of incestuous relations.
36. Scenes laid in disorderly houses.

Per cent of the budget of the French film Les Miserables *(1911) paid to secure the rights of Victor Hugo's novel*

SHAKESPEARE ON SCREEN

Literary adaptations are particularly popular among filmmakers but despite the success of *Harry Potter* (2001) and *The Lord of the Rings* (2001), William Shakespeare holds the record for being the most filmed author. At the last count, a total of 394 feature films and TV movies based on plays by William Shakespeare have been made. Shakespeare makes it onto the silver screen not just in straight adaptations of his plays but also in films based loosely on his original premise, such as *West Side Story* (1961). There are also the occasional 'life of Shakespeare' films such as *Shakespeare in Love* (1998). *Hamlet* has appealed most to filmmakers with 75 versions, followed by *Romeo and Juliet with* 51 and *Macbeth*, which has been filmed 33 times.

QUOTE UNQUOTE

Cinema is the most beautiful fraud in the world
Jean-Luc Godard, French filmmaker

A YEAR IN THE MOVIES

The January Man (1989)
15 Février 1839 (2001)
The Wedding March (1928)
The April Fools (1969)
Maytime (1937)
June Bride (1948)
Born on the Fourth of July (1989)
The Teahouse of the August Moon (1956)
September Storm (1960)
The Hunt for Red October (1990)
Sweet November (2001)
A Warm December (1973)

NELLY THE SPACESHIP

Films can use some unusual sounds to generate the sound effect desired:
• In *Star Wars* (1977), the sound of a TIE fighter was concocted by mixing the squeal of a young elephant with the sound of a passing car driving on a rain-covered motorway.
• The scream of the demon being exorcised from the child in *The Exorcist* (1973) was a recording of squealing pigs being driven to slaughter.
• The dinosaur noises in *Jurassic Park* (1993) were a combination of the screams of a dolphin, the hiss of a goose and the hoot of a mating tortoise.

IT JUST GOES TO SHOW...

Some kids turn out just as you expect...

Meg Ryan was voted cutest girl in her class
Michael Caine was nicknamed the professor
Billy Crystal was voted wittiest student in his class
Sandra Bullock was voted most likely to brighten your day

...and others surprise you

Robin Williams was voted least likely to succeed
Tom Cruise was voted least likely to succeed
Kate Winslet's nickname was 'blubber'
Steven Spielberg was called 'the retard'

SILVER-SCREEN SCRAWLINGS

I was three years old. Nobody had told me what a cinema or a film was, and certainly nothing about the concept of an animated cartoon; and I was taken into the largest enclosed space I'd ever seen, into a crowd of strangers, put on a seat, and the lights went out. Figures fifteen feet high loomed over me. The film was *Snow White*; and I felt my sanity slipping until the moment when the queen metamorphosed into the witch. Then I screamed and screamed, and could not stop. My mother called an usherette to have me removed, and I was handed into strange-smelling arms behind a bright beam that dazzled me. The arms hugged my squirming form and carried me out, while my mother stayed to watch the rest of the film. But the exit was at the foot of the screen, and I was being borne up towards that great drooling hag, away from safety, pinioned by someone I couldn't see, and the witch was laughing

Alan Garner in *Seeing in the Dark: A Compendium of Cinemagoing*

FORBIDDEN FILMS

Because of its graphic portrayal of violence and two brutal rapes, the BBFC banned ***Straw Dogs*** (1971) from being released on video and DVD from 1984 until 2002. The film came out in the same year as *A Clockwork Orange* and Ken Russell's *The Devils* and so had to contend with an atmosphere of near hysteria regarding censorship. The film received media attention because of the graphic rape scene where it appears that the victim is possibly enjoying the rape. Prominent individuals of the time including film critics Derek Malcolm and Alexander Walker and the jazz musician and film critic George Melly wrote an open letter to *The Times* in an attempt to get the film banned.

THE WIT AND WISDOM OF 007

Pussy Galore: 'My name is Pussy Galore.'
Bond: 'I must be dreaming.'
Goldfinger (1964)

Tiffany Case opens the door almost naked:
Tiffany Case: 'I'll finish dressing.'
Bond: 'Oh, please don't, not on my account.'
Diamonds Are Forever (1971)

Bond: 'Don't worry. I'm not supposed to be here either.'
Honey Ryder: 'Are you looking for shells too?'
Bond: 'No, I'm just looking.'
Dr. No (1962)

Bond is dangling from a cable car 1,000 feet up:
Dr Holly Goodhead: 'Hang on!'
Bond: 'The thought had occurred to me.'
Moonraker (1971)

Plenty O'Toole: 'Hi, I'm Plenty.'
Bond: 'But of course you are.'
Plenty O'Toole: 'Plenty O'Toole.'
Bond: 'Named after your father perhaps?'
Diamonds Are Forever (1971)

After shooting a baddie with a spear gun:
Bond: 'I think he got the point.'
Thunderball (1965)

After knocking a lamp into a bathtub to electrocute an enemy:
Bond: 'Shocking! Positively shocking!'
Goldfinger (1964)

Bond: 'Miss Anders... I didn't recognise you with your clothes on.'
The Man With The Golden Gun (1974)

Magda: 'He suggests a trade. The egg for your life.'
Bond: 'Well, I heard the price of eggs was up, but isn't that a little high?'
Octopussy (1983)

Bond: 'That's a nice little nothing you're almost wearing.'
Diamonds Are Forever (1971)

While bedding Christmas Jones:
Bond: 'I thought Christmas only came once a year...'
The World is Not Enough (1999)

ALL TOGETHER NOW

The Matrix Revolutions (2003) was the first film to open at the box office at exactly the same time around the world on 5 November, which delighted every moviegoer who had ever had to wait months for a film to be allowed out of the US. This meant that it could be seen at 6am in Los Angeles, 9am in New York, 2pm in London, 5pm in Moscow, 11pm in Tokyo, 1am in Sydney and at corresponding times in another 50 countries. Popcorn for breakfast anyone?

Percentage of American films between 1938 and 1985 that use the phrase 81
'Let's get outta here'

SECRET SINGERS

Actor	Dubbed by	Film
Ann Blyth	Gogi Grant	*Both Ends of the Candle* (1957)
Audrey Hepburn	Marni Nixon	*My Fair Lady* (1964)
Christopher Plummer	Bill Lee	*The Sound of Music* (1965)
Deborah Kerr	Marni Nixon	*The King and I* (1956)
Jean Seberg	Anita Gordon	*Paint Your Wagon* (1969)
John Kerr	Bill Lee	*South Pacific* (1958)
Larry Parks	Al Jolson	*The Jolson Story* (1946)
Natalie Wood	Marni Nixon	*West Side Story* (1961)
Rita Moreno	Leona Gordon	*The King and I* (1956)
Sophia Loren	Renata Tebaldi	*Aida* (1953)

QUOTE UNQUOTE

I don't take the movies seriously, and anyone who does is in for a headache.
Bette Davis, actress

CINEMA SNACKS ABROAD

Japan
• Bento box, comes arranged with pickled plums, sushi slices, pink fish cakes and baked tofu
• Chicken legs, fried noodles and salted beef from a vending machine
• Octopus balls
• Dried, salted, chewy fish snacks
• Coffee

Mexico
• Lime and chilli sauce for popcorn

Thailand
• Sour mango with chilli and salt

Taiwan
• Sweet, salted, chocolate and strawberry-flavoured popcorn
• Dried squid
• Meatballs

• Dried tofu
• Chicken legs
• Smoothies in mango, black tea or coffee flavours

Brazil
• Cheese balls

India
• Sprouted beans in a tomato and chilli paste mix

Mexico
• Chilli served with mango or tamarind (a sour, tart fruit)
• 'Dedo Indy' or 'Indy Finger' made of chilli, tamarind and sugar

Colombia
• Grape-flavoured fizzy drink
• A mixed flavoured cherry and watermelon drink

VEHICLE VIEWING

American film-fan Richard M Hollingshead invented the drive-in movie in the early 1930s. He experimented with a projector and a car in his back garden until he was satisfied that he had a working idea. He then went down to the patent office and received US patent number 1-909-537 on 16 May 1932.

The first drive-in was in Hollingshead's home state of New Jersey and was opened in June 1933. From there the idea really took off and spread across the US. By 1942 there were 95 drive-ins across the US. The war slowed down the popularity of drive-ins as petrol and rubber for tyres were both heavily rationed. However, once the war was over, drive-in openings skyrocketed and by 1948 there were 820.

The baby boom gave drive-ins a boost, as a new generation of teenagers became the perfect audience. By the beginning of the 1950s there were food stalls, playgrounds and afternoon entertainment hours before the main feature started.

By 1958 there were almost 5,000 drive-in theatres in the US. The biggest drive-in in Michigan could accommodate 3,000 cars.

The entertainment of the film was no longer enough and a trip to the drive-in became a family experience as various venues offered different activities such as miniature trains, pony rides, boat rides, talent shows, miniature golf and animal shows.

The 1970s and 1980s saw a huge decline in the numbers of drive-ins and many closed as the number of homes enjoying VCRs and cable TV grew. The 1990s saw a slight renaissance of the drive-in but they never regained the popularity they once enjoyed.

ON-SCREEN CHEMISTRY

According to a survey carried out by the Royal Society of Chemistry in 2004, the following couples demonstrated the strongest attraction on screen:

1. Spencer Tracy and Katharine Hepburn – *Adam's Rib* (1949) and *Guess Who's Coming To Dinner* (1967)

2. Elizabeth Taylor and Richard Burton – *Cleopatra* (1963) and *Who's Afraid of Virginia Woolf?* (1966)

3. Humphrey Bogart and Lauren Bacall – *The Big Sleep* (1946) and *Key Largo* (1948)

4. Mel Gibson and Danny Glover – *Lethal Weapon* series (1987, 1989, 1992 and 1998)

5. Robert Redford and Paul Newman – *Butch Cassidy and the Sundance Kid* (1969) and *The Sting* (1973)

MIXED-UP MOVIE STARS

Unscramble these famous actors
STORY BLUNDER • NATIVE NODDY
REVIEW AGONY SURE
Answer on page 153.

TOP 10 GROSSING FILMS
BY UK DIRECTORS

Film	Director	Birth Place	Year
1. *Star Wars: Episode VI – Return of the Jedi*	Richard Marquand	Cardiff	1983
2. *Gladiator*	Ridley Scott	South Shields	2000
3. *The Bodyguard*	Mick Jackson	Aveley	1992
4. *Hannibal*	Ridley Scott	South Shields	2001
5. *American Beauty*	Sam Mendes	Reading	1999
6. *Top Gun*	Tony Scott	Stockton-on-Tees	1986
7. *Indecent Proposal*	Adrian Lyne	Peterborough	1993
8. *Fatal Attraction*	Adrian Lyne	Peterborough	1987
9. *Beverly Hills Cop II*	Tony Scott	Stockton-on-Tees	1987
10. *Saturday Night Fever*	John Badham	Luton	1977

QUOTE UNQUOTE

*It's like being assaulted by a gang of singing cherubs
wielding sticks of candyfloss.*
Cosmo Landesman, *The Times* film writer, on *Love Actually*

WORDS ON FILM

The first public showing of what many Catholics view as Martin Scorsese's outrageous interpretation of the Biblical epic drew both predictable and highly unpredictable howls...

What was unpredictable was about the protest was a devastatingly subversive counter protest by a small group who said they were present 'on behalf of the acolytes of Our Lady of Ballinspittle' and who said they wanted to 'protect the rights of blasphemers and heretics and Nobel prize winning great novelists'...

The protesters carried placards saying things like : 'Jesus, in Him there is no sin', 'It's a sin to go in' and 'It is the work of the devil'. Those protesting against the protesters had placards stating 'Mary Mag was a Hag' and 'Jesus was nailed not screwed.'

Des O'Sullivan, *The Cork Examiner*

BIG BIG SCREEN

The largest cinema in the world is the Radio City Music Hall, New York City, which has 5,910 seats. Originally known as 'The Showplace of the Nation,' the cinema opened on 27 December 1932. Its auditorium measures 160 feet from back to stage and the ceiling is 84 high. Radio City Music Hall premiered its first film, *The Bitter Tea of General Yen* (1933), soon after the building opened. Since 1933 more than 700 films have opened at the cinema. They include *King Kong* (1933); *White Christmas* (1954); *Breakfast at Tiffany's* (1961); *To Kill a Mockingbird* (1962); *Mary Poppins* (1964); *101 Dalmatians* (1964); and *The Lion King* (1994). Cary Grant, Ginger Rogers, and Katharine Hepburn have taken Radio City box office prizes for the number of films screened there. All three had more than 22 of their films shown at the Hall. Films have not been given such prominence at the cinema in recent years, although the Music Hall still premieres selected films. However, it is best known for hosting popular concerts, stage shows, special attractions and media events.

BIG SCREEN BEASTIES

Name: Terry

Breed: Cairn Terrier

Film: *The Wizard of Oz* (1939)

Trivia: The casting department were given a copy of the original book by L Frank Baum and told to find a dog that matched WW Denslow's illustrations. This proved difficult as no one recognised the breed of dog in the pictures. It was eventually decided that the dog was a cairn terrier and a suitable one was tracked down and offered $125 a week.

The diminutive canine star performed well, although she did have a few problems with the powerful wind machines used on set, which regularly blew her over.

Terry had her name officially changed to Toto after *The Wizard of Oz* came out.

She went on to star in 11 Hollywood films, including *Twin Beds* (1942), in which she was reunited with the Wicked Witch of the West, Margaret Hamilton.

QUOTE UNQUOTE

Even if I set out to make a film of a fillet of sole,
it would be about me.
Fedérico Fellini, Italian filmmaker

Olivia de Havilland (1916–) and Joan Fontaine (1917–)

'I married first, won the Oscar before Olivia did, and if I die first, she'll undoubtedly be livid because I beat her to it!'
Joan Fontaine

The sibling rivalry between de Havilland and Fontaine goes right back to their childhood. It has been reported that their mother, actress Lillian Fontaine, set her daughters against one another to spur them on to better success.

The first time the rivalry became public was after the 1941 Oscar ceremony when the sisters were both nominated for the best actress award. Olivia was up for *Hold Back the Dawn* (1941) and Joan was up for *Suspicion* (1941). Joan won.

Olivia was the first to achieve success as an actress and had apparently always displayed a 'superior attitude' towards Joan. However, Joan has been the one to speak more openly to the press about the rivalry.

The press and the film studios were more than happy to fan the flames of the sisters' feud. Many people said that Joan was the prettier of the two, but that Olivia was the better actress. This opinion could be said to have been proven by Olivia's two Oscars for *To Each His Own* (1946) and *The Heiress* (1949) versus Joan's single one for *Suspicion* (1941).

The rivalry became so bad that by 1947, when Olivia won the best actress award for *To Each His Own* (1946), Olivia refused to acknowledge Joan when she tried to congratulate her.

When their domineering matriarch of a mother died in 1975, there were more icy silences at the memorial service. They never spoke again.

In 1978 Joan published her memoirs, *No Bed Of Roses,* which included her account of the highlights of the family feud, did nothing to bring about a reconciliation. In 1979, they both attended the 50th anniversary of the Academy Awards but refused to speak and had to be seated at opposite ends of the stage. Olivia has settled in Paris and Joan in New York but they have no plans to speak ever again. As Joan has said: 'We've not spoken since Mother's death in 1975, and that's it, kid. Never again'.

BABY ON TOP

Ronald LeRoy Overaker, better known as Baby LeRoy, was the top star in *A Bedtime Story* (1933). He was six months old and so the youngest person to ever get top billing in a film. He starred in nine films between 1933 and 1935 before retiring from films altogether at the grand old age of four. His milk was reportedly once spiked with gin by WC Fields.

Year, in the twentieth century, when Crocodile Dundee *was released, it became the highest grossing film in the US made outside of the US*

Since reaching adulthood and being cruelly dropped by Disney, Simba had difficulty finding work.

WORDS ON FILM

For Mrs Ruggles did not approve of cinemas, especially for the young. 'You're far better plying in the street or the Park,' was the invariable reply when approached for pennies for Mickey Mouse. 'Dirty stuffy places – full of germs and most of what they show unfit for children anyway.' Very occasionally – on birthdays and Bank Holidays – was she known to relent. Jo, however had one grown up friend who shared his enthusiasm and sometimes gave him halfpennies, and this was Mrs. Hare next-door-but-one. She was a cleaner at the Majestic Cinema, the second largest in the Town, and, although his mother said she was a rotten one and no place but a cinema where it was mostly dark would employ her, to Jo she was a most romantic and thrilling person. She knew the coming programmes almost before the manager himself, and could tell one stories of all the stars, even of Mickey Mouse, and had a free pass for herself and her husband once a week.

Jo was consumed with jealousy of her husband, and would dream day-dreams of how, when he was grown up, he would murder Mr. Hare, and share the free pass for life.

Eve Garnett,
The Family at One End Street

LIGHTS, CAMERA...LOVE!

Couple: Susan Sarandon and Tim Robbins
Film: *Bull Durham* (1988)
Love story: Sarandon and Robbins have been together – but not married – since the two met on the set of the 1988 baseball film *Bull Durham*. The pair worked together again on *Dead Man Walking* (1995), the death-row drama starring Sarandon and directed by Robbins. They have two children together: Jack Henry and Miles Guthrie.

Couple: Annette Bening and Warren Beatty
Film: *Bugsy* (1991)
Love story: At the time, Bening was thought to be just another conquest for serial womaniser Beatty. The couple have stayed together despite his reputation and his opinions on relationships such as 'My notion of a wife at 40 is that a man should be able to change her, like a bank note, for two twenties.' They have four children together.

Couple: Lauren Bacall and Humphrey Bogart
Film: *To Have And To Have Not* (1944)
Love story: Bogart and Bacall met and fell in love on set. The director, Howard Hawks, later said that he thought Bogart fell in love with the character that Bacall was playing, Marie 'Slim' Browning, and so she had to play that character for the rest of her life. Bogart was married three times before Bacall, although it was her first marriage. The couple had two children before Bogart died in 1957.

MOVIEGOERS BEWARE

Because of the size of the screen, the excellent sound quality and lack of possible distractions, watching a movie exposes the moviegoer to an intense visual journey that can have a variety of effects on body and mind. During exciting or emotionally charged scenes, there is a notable heart rate acceleration as well as increased sweating and nervous behaviour (biting nails, playing with hair, tapping feet). Exposure to certain films can also trigger epileptic attacks in susceptible individuals. Eyestrain can be a problem when attending double bills; a break of at least 10 minutes every hour is recommended to rest the eyes and prevent any back injuries due to bad posture. When it comes to scary movies, long-term consequences in children and adults can include problems such as sleeplessness, permanent anxiety and fear of the dark. The unwholesome snacks sold in cinemas could also lead to obesity.

THE ORIGINS OF BRITAIN'S CINEMAS

Odeon: The first Odeon cinema was opened in 1930 in Perry Bar, Birmingham by Oscar Deutsch, who is often wrongly described as a German immigrant but was actually the son of a Hungarian immigrant. Another common misperception is that Deutsch invented the name Odeon (an acronym for Oscar Deutsch Entertains the Nation). In fact, there had been Odeon cinemas and theatres in Europe before; Deutsch's publicity team simply came up with the acronym to promote Deutsch Odeons. Between 1930 and Deutsch's early death in 1941, 258 Odeon cinema buildings were erected throughout Britain. The modern architecture and interior design of these Picture Palaces changed the face of both urban and rural Britain. Upon Deutsch's death, Odeon Cinemas were sold to J Arthur Rank.

ABC: By the late 1930s Associated British Cinemas operated around 460 cinemas in Britain (many of them called Rex, Savoy, or Regal) making it the country's biggest player in film exhibition. Unlike Odeon, ABC didn't rely quite as heavily on cinema construction but acquired a lot of its theatres by reconstructing existing buildings.

Gaumont-British: Gaumont-British, the third major British cinema company, started as a subsidiary of Gaumont, the French film production company that dominated large parts of the European film industry before World War One. By the late 1930s Gaumont-British operated over 300 cinemas in Britain. Its theatres mainly offered 'cine-variety', which meant that there would also be a full variety performance including dancers, comedians, cartoons and newsreel presentations.

STUDIO SUMMARIES

Warner Brothers

Logo: the WB letters in a shield

Key facts: The Warner brothers Jack, Sam, Harold and Albert founded their studio in 1923. Its initial financial struggles were alleviated by the success of their first star, Rin Tin Tin, a German Shepherd dog who became the world's biggest box office draw by 1926. The animal actor's popular films are said to have saved the company from bankruptcy. The 1927 film *The Jazz Singer* was their first talking picture and was an instant success. In 1930 Warner Brothers began producing cartoons, leading to the creation of characters such as Daffy Duck, Bugs Bunny and Tweety Pie. Warner Brothers were the first studio to screen a coloured newsreel in 1948.

NO TANTRUMS PLEASE

Director Steven Soderbergh knows how to get what he wants. Despite having worked with the likes of Michael Douglas, George Clooney and Julia Roberts and having won the Oscar for best director for *Traffic* (2000), he was still on a tight budget for *Full Frontal* (2002). So much so that he had to make some unusual demands of his stars. Although Hollywood movers and shakers are reputed to care only about the size of their trailer and the size of their name on the film poster, some were persuaded by Soderbergh's unusual approach. With a mere $2 million to make the film, each person involved with the film was given the following list:

- All sets are practical locations.
- You will drive yourself to the set. If you are unable to drive yourself, a driver will pick you up, but you will probably become the subject of ridicule. Either way, you must arrive alone.
- There will be no craft service, so you should arrive on set 'having had'. Meals will vary in quality.
- You will pick, provide, and maintain your own wardrobe.
- You will create and maintain your own hair and make-up.
- There will be no trailers. The company will attempt to provide holding areas near a given location, but don't count on it. If you need to be alone a lot, you're pretty much screwed.
- Improvisation will be encouraged.
- You will be interviewed about your character. This material may end up in the film.
- You will be interviewed about the other characters. This material may end up in the finished film.
- You will have fun whether you want to or not. If any of these guidelines are problematic for you, stop reading now and send this screenplay back where it came from.

Despite the decidedly un-glamorous approach, Soderbergh's rules caught the imagination of David Duchovny, Catherine Keener, Julia Roberts and Brad Pitt among others, who all became members of the *Full Frontal* cast.

MIXED-UP MOVIE STARS

Unscramble these famous actors
SLOVENLY STEEL STAR • HMM, A SNOT POEM
DEAR, DEAR RUDE PIG
Answer on page 153.

HOLLYWOOD STUDIOS

20th Century Fox

Logo: the studio's name as part of a city's skyline, surrounded by searchlights. It is accompanied by the legendary fanfare.

Key facts: In 1935, Fox Film merged with Twentieth Century Pictures, creating 20th Century Fox. William Fox was forced out of the company during the merger by Sidney Kent, who took over leadership of the newly formed corporation.

Fox Film held the patents of the Movietone sound system that made the recording of sound on film possible. Their biggest films include *Star Wars* (1977), *Die Hard* (1988), *Home Alone* (1990) and *Independence Day* (1996).

FILM WATCHING FEARS

Thaasophobia ....an abnormal and persistent fear of sitting or being idle

Nyctophobia ....an abnormal fear of the night or darkness

Anthropophobia ....an abnormal and persistent fear of people or society

Claustrophobia ....a fear of closed spaces, or of being closed in

Demophobia ....a fear of being in crowded places

Social phobia ....a fear of being around unfamiliar people in social situations

Xenophobia ....a fear of strangers

Photophobia ....a fear of light

Ligyrophobia ....a fear of loud noises

Genuphobia ....an abnormal and persistent fear of knees

THE KID STAYS IN THE PICTURE

Macaulay Culkin (1980–)

Macaulay Culkin's wealth has been estimated to be in the region of $17 million. He reportedly earned $100,000 for *Home Alone* (1990), followed by the considerably larger sum of $4,500,000 for *Home Alone 2: Lost in New York* (1992) and a huge $8,000,000 for *Getting Even with Dad* (1994).

His launch pad was the surprise success of *Home Alone* (1990), which became the biggest grossing film of the year worldwide.

He got married at 18 but divorced two years later.

He famously burnt out at the age of 14, although he returned to film acting in 2003 and appeared in a couple of films.

He is also the godfather of Michael Jackson's first child.

The films that had kept us excited for weeks in advance were a twenty minute short on yodelling in the Swiss Alps, and a half hour documentary about the Austrian people engaged in one of their favourite pastimes, skiing. It was almost as thrilling as the day we rioted over the high price of water and broke the settlement manager's windows. Men, women and children were sitting huddled together, watching the strange antics of the whites as they walked on snow, somersaulted through the air, almost always landed on their skis. At every jump on the slopes a uniformly sharp intake of breath was heard from the crowd. Sometimes when the move appeared to be particularly daring we, the women, clapped heartily whilst the men slapped each other on the back with unbridled gusto as though the skier's accomplishment was their own personal victory. When, now and again, the skiers tumbled down, legs splayed, staring red-faced into the eye of the camera and into our faces, we burst out laughing at these Europeans frolicking in the snow, while we sat in the heat of our night.

Nancee Oku Bright in *Seeing in the Dark:*
A Compendium of Cinemagoing

QUOTE UNQUOTE

The only thing worse than watching a bad movie is being in one.
Elvis Presley, US singer and actor

FATTY ARBUCKLE

Born Roscoe Conkling Arbuckle, this actor is mainly remembered for his involvement in a murder trial. Arbuckle was a well-established comic actor in silent films, and after his film *Dollar A Year Man* (1921) he signed a three-year deal with Paramount that would have made him the first film star to be paid $1 million a year. In the same year, Arbuckle held a party at his house. One of the guests was a largely unknown film actress called Virginia Rappe who was at the time engaged to actor and director Henry Lehrman. There was much merry making and drinking at the party and Rappe fell seriously ill and died a few days later of a ruptured bladder. Rumours abounded that her death was a result of 'amorous advances' by Arbuckle and he was subsequently charged with rape and murder. He was tried three times, and was eventually acquitted in 1923. However his career was damaged beyond repair and he was the first star to be banned from acting after being blacklisted by Hollywood producers. He turned to directing under the pseudonym William Goodrich and agreed a deal with Warner Brothers in 1933. However, in a cruel twist of fate he died of a heart attack at the age of 46 on the day he would have signed the contract to enable his return to the screen.

QUOTE ME HAPPY

David Manning was the fictitious journalist invented by Sony (mother company of Columbia Pictures) to write rave reviews about their films, producing bite-sized quotes that were used on film posters. In June 2001, *Newsweek* reporter John Horn followed up the quotes supposedly taken from reviews written for the Ridgefield Press. Horn found that the editorial office had never employed a reviewer by the name of David Manning. Allegedly, an anonymous Sony executive made up David Manning in June 2000 to boost the promotional impact of film advertising, but it remains unclear if others were involved in the affair.

The phoney quotes included for *The Animal* (2001): 'The producing team of Big Daddy has delivered another winner!' and describing Heath Ledger in *A Knight's Tale* (2001) as 'this year's hottest new star'.

FOREIGN LANGUAGE FILMS IN THE UK

Film	Year	Language	Total UK Gross (£)
Crouching Tiger, Hidden Dragon	2001	Mandarin	9,356,176
Amélie	2001	French	4,942,157
Life is Beautiful	1999	Italian	3,083,174
Kabhi Khushi Kabhie Gham	2001	Hindi	2,498,281
Cyrano de Bergerac	1991	French	2,458,175
Monsoon Wedding	2002	Hindi/Punjabi	2,059,532
Kuch Kuch Hota Hai	1998	Hindi	1,750,000
Devdas	2002	Hindi	1,663,692
Farewell My Concubine	1994	Mandarin	1,639,622
Il Postino	1994	Italian	1,292,525

GETTING AWAY FROM IT ALL

In 2002, inventor Angus MacFarlan tackled the perennial problem of mobile phones in cinemas by building a 17-foot mobile cinema for two. MacFarlan considers people talking, laughing at the wrong moments and mobile phones as unacceptable distractions during the watching of a film. In his self proclaimed 'smallest cinema in the world' people are stripped of their mobile phones before they can sit down. However, he does allow ushers, ice cream, popcorn and advertisements. MacFarlan admits that a full cinema audience can enhance the watching of comedies, but romance and horror films benefit from his considerably more intimate surroundings. Which leaves only the question of why he needs an usher for a two-person cinema.

Age of Lillian Gish in The Whales of August *(1987), the oldest actress in a leading role in a film*   93

THE REVISED SCRIPT WAS BETTER

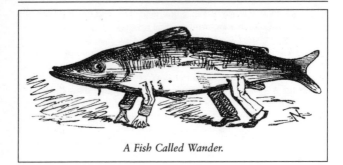

A Fish Called Wander.

WORDS ON FILM

I could never get over the transformation of the vast auditorium by the dimming of the lights, the beautiful changes of colour on the curtains, and the anticipation brought on by the roaring lion, the muscle man with his gong, the snow capped mountains, the searchlights probing the 20th Century. That moment seems in retrospect to have been more exciting than any of the films that followed. The 20th Century Fox logo always made me think we were about to see a war film, as the searchlight that had woken us in London in the blitz always preceded an air-raid. Even in peace time Exeter, bombed London, in reality and on the newsreels, was hard to dislodge from my mind.

Roland Miller in *Seeing in the Dark:*
A Compendium of Cinemagoing*

FIVE GO TO THE MOVIES

In American films any phone numbers in the script almost always start with 555 for which there is a simple explanation. Thirty years ago when the use of exchange names was still popular in the USA, the dials on telephones had letters as well as numbers, and telephone numbers were often a combination of letters and numbers: for example; STate (78). The '5' key corresponds to the letters 'j', 'k' and 'l' and it is impossible to make a place name starting with any combination of those letters. The '5' key was therefore never assigned any real numbers. When real phone numbers were bombarded after featuring in a film, producers were encouraged to use numbers that had no real life equivalent and so the 555 tradition was born.

HOW TO SURVIVE A HORROR MOVIE

Ever wondered why people in horror films are so stupid? If only they would follow some simple rules...

1. Never drink or do drugs – and stay a virgin.
2. Never tell the group that you'll be right back.
3. Always make sure that your car has a brand new battery so it will start immediately in times of crisis such as being pursued by a monster/zombie/unhinged jilted lover.
4. When searching a house for danger, turn the lights on.
5. If you're running away, expect to trip or fall down at least twice, more if you are of the female persuasion.
6. Big breasts and blonde hair are a death-wish.
7. As a general rule, don't solve puzzles that open portals to hell.
8. Do not search the basement, especially if the power has just gone out.
9. Always check the back seat of your car before you get in.
10. Anniversary nights of executions, horrible murders, or terrifying rituals should be viewed with fear. Especially if you are on the spot where the event took place. And certainly if you or a friend is somehow descended from one of the original participants.
11. Kill the person in the group who suggests that you split up. They will eventually get you killed.
12. Slap the screaming hysterical girl, she will be the one to distract everyone when there really is danger.
13. Nothing is ever over if it is still night time.
14. Take heed of all warnings from animals and children. They have an uncanny ability to sense danger.
15. Never publicly announce your plans for the future if you make it out alive. It guarantees your impending grizzly death.
16. Never, under any circumstances, run upstairs if you are being chased.
17. When it appears that you have killed the monster/axe murderer, never check to see if it's really dead.
18. Listen closely to the soundtrack. If the music starts getting tense when you open a door, close it. Turn around. Run away. Fast.
19. Never watch a horror movie while you're in a horror movie.
20. Never say 'Who's there?' It will almost certainly be something you don't want to meet.

Taken from, and with gratitude to, an anonymous posting on the internet.

LIGHTS, CAMERA...LOVE!

Couple: Uma Thurman and Ethan Hawke

Film: *Gattaca* (1997)

Love story: On the *Gattaca* set, Uma was 'enchanted' by the teen heartthrob of *Dead Poets Society* (1989). She had already been married for two years to actor Gary Oldman (12 years her senior), but was divorced when she met Ethan. The couple married in 1998 by which time Uma was already expecting their first child. The couple had two children, Maya and Roan before filing for divorce in 2003.

Couple: Tom Hanks and Rita Wilson

Film: *Volunteers* (1985)

Love story: When the couple met on set Tom was hitched to high school sweetheart Samantha Lewes and Rita was engaged. The duo quickly realised they were destined to be together and have since found fame and fortune as one of Hollywood's most powerful couples. They married in 1988 and have two children, Chester and Truman.

Couple: Tom Cruise and Nicole Kidman

Film: *Days of Thunder* (1990)

Love story: They met on the set of *Days of Thunder* (1990) while Tom was still married to Mimi Rogers. They divorced and Tom and Nicole were married by the end of that year. They adopted two children, Isabella and Connor. Once thought to be one of the strongest Hollywood marriages, the couple split in 2001 after a decade of marriage and after acting together in *Far and Away* (1992) and *Eyes Wide Shut* (1999).

AN ALL-AMERICAN LOVE AFFAIR

Top importers of US films in 1999

Country	No of films imported
Lebanon	455
Spain	216
Canada	204
Mexico	203
Republic of Korea	200
Iceland	158
Nicaragua	140
Germany	134
Panama	134
New Zealand	133

96 *Year, in the nineteenth century, when the first screen kiss was performed in the aptly named* The Kiss

TOP 20 WOMEN'S FILMS

Dirty Dancing (1987)
Bridget Jones's Diary (2001)
Thelma and Louise (1991)
Steel Magnolias (1989)
Breakfast at Tiffany's (1961)
The Piano (1993)
Titanic (1997)
Gone with the Wind (1939)
From Here to Eternity (1953)
When Harry Met Sally... (1989)
Truly, Madly, Deeply (1991)
Fried Green Tomatoes (1991)
Ghost (1990)
The Bridges of Madison County (1995)
The Color Purple (1985)
Little Women (1994)
Shakespeare in Love (1998)
True Romance (1993)
Out of Africa (1985)
Grease (1978)

According to the 14,000 people who answered a 2004 UK
supermarket online survey

QUOTE UNQUOTE

*That was my one big Hollywood hit, but, in a way, it hurt my
picture career. After that, I was typecast as a lion, and there just
weren't many parts for lions.*
Bert Lahr, the cowardly lion in *The Wizard of Oz*

FILM STARS AND THEIR ANCESTORS

Sir John Gielgud: Ellen Terry
(revered Shakespearean stage actress, 1847–1928)
Glenn Ford: Martin van Buren (8th President of the USA 1837–1841)
Helena Bonham Carter: Herbert Asquith
(British Prime Minister 1908–1916)
Judy Garland: Ulysses S Grant (18th President of the USA 1869–1877)
Joyce Grenfell: Nancy Astor
(first woman to take a seat in the House of Commons)
William Holden: Warren G Harding
(29th President of the USA 1921–1923)
Errol Flynn: Fletcher Christian
(famous for his part in the mutiny on the Bounty)

MOST EXPENSIVE PIECES OF
FILM MEMORABILIA

Item and sale	Price (£)
1. David O Selznick's Oscar for *Gone with the Wind* (1939) Sotheby's, New York, 1999 *(bought by Michael Jackson)*	954,104
2. Judy Garland's ruby slippers from *The Wizard of Oz* (1939) Christie's, New York, 2000	453,815
3. Bette Davis's Oscar for *Jezebel* (1938) Christie's, New York, 2001 *(bought by Steven Spielberg)*	407,407
4. Vivien Leigh's Oscar for *Gone with the Wind* (1939) Sotheby's, New York, 1993	378,737
5. Clark Gable's Oscar for *It Happened One Night* (1934) Christie's, Los Angeles, 1996	366,770
6. Statue from *The Maltese Falcon* (1941) Christie's Rockefeller, New York, 1994	255,580
7. James Bond's Aston Martin DB5 from *Goldfinger* (1964) Sotheby's, New York, 1986	179,915
8. James Bond's Aston Martin DB5 from *GoldenEye* (1995) Christie's, London, 2001	157,750
9. Herman J Mankiewicz's Oscar for co-writing *Citizen Kane* (1941) Christie's, New York, 1999	150,721
10. Clark Gable's personal script for *Gone with the Wind* (1939) Christie's, Los Angeles, 1996	147,614

QUOTE UNQUOTE

I'm not very keen on Hollywood.
I'd rather have a nice cup of cocoa really.
Noël Coward, playwright, writer, actor

Movieland is so much better than living in the real world when...

Travelling in a car – don't worry about using the seat belt, you are immune to the laws of gravity.

Locking a car – no one will steal the car (unless this is central to the plot).

Reloading weapons – don't worry, the weapon doesn't require any extra ammunition and will fire continuously. In the unlikely situation that you do run out of ammunition, you will be able to use the empty gun to knock someone out, usually in a comical manner.

Parking your car – you will always be able to get a space in front of the building you want to visit without having to find a meter or check the parking restrictions.

Taking on a large group of martial arts experts – they will patiently wait until you have dealt with them one by one, then inadequately try and fight you.

Talking on the phone – you don't need to worry about saying hello or goodbye. The person on the other end of the line knows when the conversation is over and won't think that you've hung up on them.

Running from an enemy – there will always be a convenient street parade taking place in which you can take refuge.

Escaping from a building – you can always fit into a nice, clean ventilation system that goes everywhere in the building.

Outrunning an explosion – even though an explosion travels at around 13,640mph and even world-class athletes can only manage around 23mph, you will be able to escape the blast.

Shaving – even if you are interrupted while shaving and have to wipe off the remaining foam, the rest of your face will be perfectly clean-shaven.

Eating Chinese food – you will never have trouble using chopsticks.

Ordering drinks in a bar – even if you have never been to the bar before you can order a generic drink such as 'beer' and the bartender will not question which brand you want. And you never need to wait for change.

Someone's about to shoot you – don't worry someone else will shoot the bad guy from behind right at the last minute.

A hand lands on your shoulder – don't worry, it's never the monster or the enemy, it's just that weirdo from next door or your love interest displaying about as much tact as a sledgehammer considering you're in a horror/thriller film.

FORBIDDEN FILMS

The Life of Brian (1979) premiered in New York in August 1979. The Catholic film-monitoring office quickly rated the film 'C' for 'Condemned' and urged Catholics not to visit cinemas where it was playing, as it was a sin to do so. In England, the film was rated 15 and approved for national release uncut. However, The Church of England Board for Social Responsibility began campaigning against the film through the Festival of Light by circulating negative literature and encouraging Christians to pray for the film's downfall. When it was released in Britain in early 1980 it was censored by local councils on health and safety grounds, which led Michael Palin to wonder: 'if they thought it would spread diseases in cinemas'.

Life of Brian was banned in Harrogate, parts of Surrey, east Devon and Cornwall and remained banned in Swansea until 1997, when it was permitted to be shown in cinemas in aid of Comic Relief.

WORDS ON FILM

They arrived at the Princess Circle Lobby. They walked past the Refreshment Counter where the orangedrinks were waiting. And the lemondrinks were waiting. The orange too orange. The lemon too lemon. The chocolates too melty.

The Torch Man opened the heavy Princess Circle door into the fan-whirring, peanut-crunching darkness. It smelled of breathing people and hairoil. And old carpets. A magical, *Sound of Music* smell that Rahel remembered and treasured. Smells, like music, hold memories. She breathed deeply, and bottled it up for posterity.

Estha had the tickets. Little man. He lived in a cara-van. Dum dum.

The Torch Man shone his light on the pink tickets. Row J. Numbers 17,18,19,20. Estha, Amma, Rahel, Baby Kocham-ma. They squeezed past irritated people who moved their legs this way and that to make space. The seats of the chairs had to be pulled down. Baby Kochamma held Rahel's seat down while she climbed on. She wasn't heavy enough, so the chair folded her into itself like sandwich stuffing, and she watched from between her knees. Two knees and a fountain. Estha, with more dignity than that, sat on the edge of his chair.

The shadows of the fans were on the sides of the screen where the picture wasn't.

Off with the torch. On with the World Hit.

The camera soared up in the skyblue (car-coloured) Austrian sky with the clear, sad sound of the church bells.

Arundhati Roy,
The God of Small Things

TOP 10 MOST SUCCESSFUL ANIMATED FILMS

Film	Year	Worldwide Total Gross ($)
The Lion King	1994	771,900,000
Monsters, Inc	2001	529,000,000
Aladdin	1992	502,400,000
Toy Story 2	1999	485,800,000
Shrek	2001	477,000,000
Tarzan	1999	449,400,000
Ice Age	2002	366,300,000
A Bug's Life	1998	363,400,000
Toy Story	1995	361,500,000
Dinosaur	2000	356,100,000

All except *Shrek* (Dreamworks SKG) and *Ice Age* (Fox Animation) are Disney films.

SIX IS THE MAGIC NUMBER

The moviegoers' game 'Six Degrees of Kevin Bacon' was inspired by the play and film by John Guare, *Six Degrees of Separation* (1993), which expounded the theory is that any two people in the world can be linked by six (or less) degrees of separation. Three students from Pennsylvania took the idea to another level for movie fans by theorising that all actors can be linked by a maximum of six steps to Kevin Bacon, who appears to be the centre of the (cinematic) universe. Although Bacon has never been a big box office draw or a favourite leading man, he has been in several ensemble casts and has appeared in numerous films since the early 1980s.

You can supposedly link Bacon to any actor in six or less steps and the fewer steps you take, the better you are at the game. For example to link Kevin Bacon to Kevin Costner takes only one step: Both were in *JFK* (1991). Julia Louis-Dreyfus from the television show Seinfeld, is not quite as simple and it takes all six steps to make a chain: She was in *Christmas Vacation* (1989) with Randy Quaid, who was in *Major League II* (1994) with Tom Berenger, who was in *Shattered* (1991) with Greta Scacchi, who was in *Presumed Innocent* (1990) with Harrison Ford, who was in *Raiders of the Lost Ark* (1981) with Karen Allen, who was in *Animal House* (1978) with Kevin Bacon. An actor can be described as having a Bacon number. Kevin Bacon himself has a Bacon number of 0. Kevin Costner has a Bacon number of 1, and Julia Louis-Dreyfus has a Bacon number of 6.

The most useful link is probably *JFK* (1991), although *A Few Good Men* (1992), *Apollo 13* (1995) and *Sleepers* (1996) are also key weapons to have at hand. And if you're a purist of the game, no television links, no relatives and no directors are allowed.

In 2003, the BBC decided to compile a poll of the worst films shown at the cinema. When they announced the results on their website (www.bbc.co.uk/films) they included some of the comments left by viewers about the films...

1. *Titanic* (1997)
– Shows that the Hollywood glitterati couldn't find their own behinds with both hands, a flashlight and a copy of Gray's *Anatomy*.
– My father fell asleep after 20 minutes. He was lucky. It was only his snoring that kept me awake.
– It sank. There. I've saved you three hours of your life.

2. *A.I.: Artificial Intelligence* (2001)
– Completely artificial but devoid of intelligence.
– Turns a promising idea into *Pinocchio on Ice*.
– All copies should be incinerated.

3. *Pearl Harbor* (2001)
– It battered my intelligence with such ferocity I could barely find my way out of the cinema.
– Made me feel unclean.

4. *Highlander II – The Quickening* (1991)
– It stank like a dead cat under my cinema chair.
– Breathtakingly stupid.

5. *The Blair Witch Project* (1999)
– Two hours that would have been more profitably spent trying to staple my tongue to my forehead.
– Gave my girlfriend motion sickness and she threw up half way through.

6. *Batman and Robin* (1997)
– I wanted to sandpaper my retinas.

7. *The Avengers* (1998)
– Made me want to drown in my own bile.
– As the film went silent before the closing credits I said aloud: 'That was ****!' and got a round of applause.

8. *Battlefield Earth* (2000)
– A totally miserable experience shared with six other sad and bemused people and 120 empty seats.

9. *Eyes Wide Shut* (1999)
– I tried to walk out of the cinema but the film had anaesthetised my legs.
– I fell asleep, even with all the bonking.
– What the hell was that all about?

10. *Vanilla Sky* (2001)
– The lowest point of my life so far.
– You recommended it. Why, Jonathan, why? (referring to film critic Jonathan Ross).
– Thanks for nothing, Jonathan.

SOUNDING IT OUT

The useful sounds that a film contains...

When a character draws a sword or a knife from a holster, it always makes a 'swish' metal-against-metal sound.

When anyone gets punched it is always accompanied by a quite satisfying but highly unrealistic 'thwack' sound that never happens in the pub on a Friday night.

When there is a martial arts fight scene, the actors' arms and legs make a swishing sound.

All spaceships/large government buildings have a woman's voice on a PA system for the 'self destruction in one minute' line.

Scenes set in London will always be accompanied by either 'Rule, Britannia' or, 'London Calling' by the Clash and Paris is always identified by accordion music and a shot of the Eiffel Tower. Anywhere in the Far East will have 'mystic' pipe music in the background.

QUOTE UNQUOTE

On the movies: It is probable that the fad will die out in the next few years
Independent (the US newspaper), 1910

MOVIE URBAN LEGENDS

Fargo

Legend: A Japanese woman died while looking for fictional buried treasure in Minnesota after watching the film *Fargo* and believing the treasure mentioned in the script was real.

The film *Fargo* opens with a claim that the story is true, which has led many to believe that a large sum of money buried by a character at the end of the film is waiting to be found. However, the claim is merely a stylistic device, as the Coen brothers, who directed and wrote the film, have admitted. At the end of the film there is the usual disclaimer that there is no resemblance to any persons living or dead. However one woman from Japan travelled to the area in winter 2001 where she was later found dead. Her death was ruled to be a suicide after a letter that she sent to her relatives was discovered in which she declared her intention to commit suicide. The rumour about the film sprang up as a result of reports that the woman had shown police officers a crude hand-drawn map and in broken English had repeated a word that sounded like 'Fargo'. Whether or not the woman really believed that she could find the *Fargo* treasure is undetermined but there seems to be some link between her death and the film.

Close Encounters of the Bird Kind.

MOVIE DOUBLE ACTS

Rock Hudson and Doris Day

Rock Hudson: (1925–1985)

Rock's name at birth was Roy Scherer, but a talent scout invented a new name for him by combining the Rock of Gibraltar and the Hudson River.

Before taking his first film role, Rock got his teeth capped and was coached intensively in acting, singing, dancing, fencing and riding. But, it still took 38 takes before he could successfully complete one line in his first film, *Fighter Squadron* (1948).

Doris Day: (1924–)

Rock Hudson called Doris Day 'Eunice' because he said that whenever he thought of her as Eunice, it made him laugh.

Day received an Oscar nomination for her role in *Pillow Talk*.

Films they made together:
Pillow Talk (1959)
Lover Come Back (1961)
Send Me No Flowers (1964)

THE MONEY MAKERS

Film	Year of release	Year of release in the UK	Country of Origin	Box Office Gross (£)
Titanic	1997	1998	US	68,989,379
Harry Potter and the Philosopher's Stone	2001	2001	US/GB	66,096,060
The Lord of the Rings: The Fellowship of the Ring	2001	2001	US/NZ	63,009,288
The Lord of the Rings: The Return of the King (still on release)	2003	2003	DL/NZ/US	59,570,599
The Lord of the Rings: The Two Towers	2002	2002	DL/NZ/US	57,600,094
Harry Potter and the Chamber of Secrets	2002	2002	US/GB/DL	54,780,731
The Full Monty	1997	1997	US/GB	52,232,058
Star Wars: Episode I – The Phantom Menace	1999	1999	US	51,063,811
Jurassic Park	1993	1993	US	47,886,423
Toy Story 2	1999	2000	US	44,306,070

MIXED-UP MOVIE STARS

Unscramble these famous actors
MERRY WARDROBE • I AM A NICE LECH
BRAIN CREEPS ON
Answer on page 153.

All of a sudden George said, "Roll 'em." No rehearsal. No nothing.

I said my first line, which was, "As you can see, my mind is made up." Within the context of the plot, that meant that I was sending my love off to Indochina without me. As I said my line, I tilted my chin the way George had told me to and waited expectantly for Clark to say his first bit of dialogue. But of course he didn't know the script. As it turned out, he didn't have to.

Instead of saying his line, he brought his face close to mine. There was a moment as he came nearer when I realised what was about to happen and I became a little lightheaded. Then he planted a terrific Gable kiss on my mouth. It was a really good, strong kiss. When he pulled away, I gulped so noticeably that I was sure the sound boom picked it up. This was really heady stuff for the kid from Inglewood. He was supposed to say something, but instead he whispered, "Go ahead, honey. What's your next line?"

"Aaah, aah, umm…" I struggled to find the words, but I felt as though I was floating. "Aaah, uh, so … so however you feel about it, aaah, I'm not going to change my mind. I'm really not going because everybody will know that there is something wrong with our being there together."

He had another line to deliver, but whatever it was, he had no intention of saying it. He leaned over and kissed me again. By this time I had no idea what was going on, except that no one had said "Cut!". While we were rolling, I knew that I wasn't supposed to look at the camera, or at George Sidney, and I certainly wasn't going to look at Carole Lombard, aka Mrs. Clark Gable, who was still out there just beyond my myopic haze.

That only left me one person to look at. As I turned to Clark Gable with a very quizzical expression, he began ad-libbing dialogue. "Tell you what, baby," he began. "Go ahead and do what you want to do, because after all, you know everything, even though you're very inexperienced."

I didn't even know what he was saying, because I could tell that another kiss was on its way. Then he kissed me *again*. This was a long kiss. Indeterminable! His lips finally left my mouth. I felt as though I were going to faint. He looked at me with his roguish smile. He had done this before. "And with that," he said, "I bid you adieu, my dear."

There was total silence.

Esther Williams with Digby Diehl
The Million Dollar Mermaid

QUOTE UNQUOTE

Our comedies are not to be laughed at.
Samuel Goldwyn, film producer

RON JEREMY

Ronald Jeremy Hyatt, born in New York on 12 March 1953, is the most famous as well as one of the most unlikely male porn stars. Despite being overweight, hairy and moustachioed, he became one of the most sought-after porn stars. His industry nickname is 'hedgehog', because of his round body shape and thick hair, but also because he has the unique ability to orally stimulate himself by rolling into a ball. He has directed over 100 films and appeared in over 1,700, including non-porn ones such as *Detroit Rock City* (1999), *54* (1998), *Ronin* (1998), *Orgazmo* (1997), *The Boondock Saints* (1999) and *Killing Zoe* (1994).

What few people know is that Jeremy holds a bachelor's degree in theatre arts as well as a master's degree in Special Education from Queen's College, New York. In 1978, his girlfriend sent his photo to *Playgirl*'s 'Boy Next Door' competition. The photo was published and Jeremy got offers from several porn producers. He entered the porn industry in its heyday and profited from the high demand for male porn actors during its Golden Era between 1975 and 1983. As the production of pornographic films was still illegal at the time, he was arrested twice but managed to escape lengthy prison sentences. In 2001, a documentary film, *Porn Star: The Legend of Ron Jeremy*, investigated the ups and downs of Jeremy's turbulent life.

MIXED-UP MOVIE STARS

Unscramble these famous actors
GERMANY • GROAN MADLY
YAWN IN ORDER
Answer on page 153.

THE KID STAYS IN THE PICTURE

Jodie Foster (1962–)

Now a major Hollywood contender, Jodie started her acting life in a commercial when she was just two years old. Her real breakthrough came in *Taxi Driver* (1976) where she played a 13-year-old prostitute.

She went on to win two Oscars for her performances in *The Accused* (1988) and *The Silence of the Lambs* (1991).

When John Warnock Hinckley Jr attempted to assassinate Ronald Reagan in 1981, he said he did it to impress Jodie after becoming obsessed with her in *Taxi Driver*.

She can now command up to $15,000,000 for appearing in a film, as she reportedly did for *Anna and the King* (1999).

THEY LOVE US
(OR AT LEAST THEY LOVE HUGH GRANT)

Top 10 importers of UK films

Country	No of films imported
Spain	47
Germany	31
New Zealand	17
Ireland	17
Denmark	16
Lithuania	16
Portugal	15
Sweden	15
Czech Republic	14
Republic of Korea	13

I'D LIKE TO THANK...

Razzies

The Golden Raspberry Awards, the award that no one wants to win, were created in 1980 to honour the bad and the ugly in film making and acting. Since the awards have started only two people have personally accepted their awards. *Showgirls* (1995) director Paul Verhoeven was the first to embrace the ceremony that most people want to avoid. *Showgirls* swept the board at the 1996 awards and Verhoeven was on hand to accept every award. Tom Green also attended the ceremony in 2002 for his universally panned *Freddy Got Fingered* (2001). The film won five awards, which Green personally accepted, including the worst screen couple for 'Tom Green and any animal he abuses'. Green took his own length of red carpet to the ceremony and unrolled it and walked along it into the tiny cinema where the awards were being held.

The actor with the most 'worst actor' wins is Sylvester Stallone who has accrued 10 awards and 30 nominations up to 2004 including worst actor of the century for '95% of everything he's ever done'.

The honour of worst actress goes to Madonna with nine awards and 15 nominations including wins for her work in *Swept Away* (2002) and *The Next Best Thing* (2000).

QUOTE UNQUOTE

People are always asking me when I'm going to retire. Why should I? I've got it two ways — I'm still making movies, and I'm a senior citizen, so I can see myself at half price.
George Burns, US comedian

BEHIND THE SCENES

Age discrimination laws meant that the director had to judge all those who auditioned for Annie *solely on ability.*

HAPPY HOUR

Film: *The Big Lebowski* (1998)

Plot: 'The Dude' lives the very happy life of a slacker in LA until he is a victim of mistaken identity and is targeted by nihilists hoping for financial reimbursement. Despite becoming involved in a saga involving women with severed toes and a kidnapping plot, not to mention having his rug peed on, The Dude manages to approach everything with a laid back attitude and a White Russian in his hand. In fact he manages to get through nine White Russians in the course of the film.

Quote: Treehorn: 'What's your drink, Dude?'

Dude: 'White Russian, thanks. How's the smut business Jackie?'

Recipe:

White Russian

2 parts vodka,

1 part coffee liqueur (such as Kahlúa)

1 part cream or milk

Mix the vodka and coffee liqueur in a glass and finish off with cream or milk. Serve over ice in a high-ball glass.

Number of the PT (patrol torpedo) boat John F Kennedy was in charge of 109
during World War Two, the experience was made into PT 109 (1963)

SSSHHHH

**Celebrities who used to work in
cinemas/theatres as ushers or usherettes**

Sylvester Stallone • Barbra Streisand
Marianne Jean-Baptiste • Charlene Tilton
George Michael • Elizabeth Garvie
George Segal • Nadia Sawalha
Jayne Irving • Kirk Douglas

CELEBRITIES WHO WERE NOT ACTORS AND THE FILMS THEY WERE IN

Paul McCartney, musician, *Eat The Rich* (1987)
Jools Holland, musician, *Spice World* (1997)
Bob Geldolf, musician, *Pink Floyd The Wall* (1982)
Tina Turner, musician, *Mad Max Beyond Thunderdome* (1985)
Pablo Picasso, artist, *The Testament of Orpheus* (1960) and
Life Begins Tomorrow (1949)
Arthur Conan Doyle, author, *The $5,000,000
Counterfeiting Plot* (1914)
Harland David 'Colonel' Sanders (of KFC), businessman,
The Big Mouth (1967)
Woodrow Wilson, politician, *The Adventures of a Boy Scout* (1915)
Gore Vidal, politician, *Bob Roberts* (1992)
Stirling Moss, racing driver, *Casino Royale* (1967)
Buzz Aldrin, astronaut, *The Boy in the Plastic Bubble* (1976)
Johnny Cash, musician, *Door to Door Maniac* (1961)

SMELL-O-VISION

'Smell-o-vision' was invented in 1960 by Mike Todd Jr, son of Mike Todd Sr, who produced *Around the World in Eighty Days* (1956), a film that took the best picture Oscar in 1957 and used Todd Senior's newly developed Todd A-O sound system. Todd Junior developed the process of Smell-o-vision, which pumped an evocative smell through pipes direct to the cinema audience's individual seats. Bottles of scent were held on a rotating drum and the process was triggered by a signal on the film itself. Only one film, *Scent of Mystery* (1960), was made in Smell-o-vision and was far from a milestone in movie history. Mike Todd Jr lost his entire investment and left the film business. Filmmaker John Waters paid homage to Smell-o-vision with his 1981 film, *Polyester*. Waters created the process of 'odorama' and, rather than pumping in scents, used individual audience 'scratch and sniff' cards.

WEIRD PLACES TO WATCH FILMS

In the dentist's chair

At a dental practice in Gloucester it is possible to watch a film on DVD while having your teeth drilled. The film is seen on DVD glasses that also block out any drilling noise. The glasses cost £300 and work through a link to a laptop or DVD player. Dentist Alex Michael says that watching a film can calm nervous patients and 'it is better for them and better for me'.

Underwater

With the release of *Finding Nemo* (2003) on DVD, diver Lloyd Scott decided that the time was right to watch an entire film underwater. Realising that holding his breath for an hour and 40 minutes was going to be a challenge, Scott kitted himself out in a full antique diving suit before descending to watch the film on an eight-by-six foot screen in a tank at the London Aquarium. The British deep-sea diver shared his viewing space with mackerels and rays. He said: 'because the animation is so lifelike, there were moments when what was on screen blended seamlessly with the underwater environment'.

At the wheel

A rather ambitious man from New York State decided that driving a car was not enough of a distraction. And so to spice up his journey he watched a film on a DVD screen inside his Mercedes. But not just any film. Thirty-five-year-old Andre Gainey popped on a porn film. He was arrested when a police officer spotted what he was doing from his unmarked car. Unfortunately for Gainey, the film was easily visible from any car following the Mercedes. He was charged with the public display of offensive material, watching a film while driving and driving with a suspended licence.

MOST PROFITABLE FILMS OF ALL TIME

Film	Year	Budget ($)	World Gross ($)
The Blair Witch Project	1999	35,000	248,662,839
American Graffiti	1973	750,000	115,000,000
Snow White and the Seven Dwarves	1937	1,488,000	187,670,866
The Rocky Horror Picture Show	1975	1,200,000	139,876,417
Rocky	1976	1,100,000	117,235,147
Gone With The Wind	1939	3,900,000	390,555,278
The Full Monty	1997	3,500,000	256,950,122
Star Wars	1977	11,000,000	797,998,007
ET – The Extra Terrestrial	1982	10,500,000	756,774,579
My Big Fat Greek Wedding	2002	5,000,000	353,906,779

WORKING TITLES

The American became *Citizen Kane* (1941)
Not Tonight Josephine! became *Some Like it Hot* (1959)
The Babysitter Murders became *Halloween* (1978)
Watch the Skies became *Close Encounters of the Third Kind* (1977)
The Greatest Gift became *It's a Wonderful Life* (1946)
Anhedonia became *Annie Hall* (1977)
$3000 became *Pretty Woman* (1990)
Star Beast became *Alien* (1979)
A Boy's Life became *ET – The Extra Terrestrial* (1982)
The Adventures of Luke Skywalker became *Star Wars* (1977)
The Beast became *King Kong* (1933)
Jesus Christ: Lust for Glory became *The Life of Brian* (1979)
Illicit Darkening became *Vertigo* (1958)
Stillness in the Water became *Jaws* (1975)
Everybody Comes to Rick's became *Casablanca* (1942)
Wise Guy became *Goodfellas* (1990)
Night Bus became *It Happened One Night* (1934)
Best Performance became *All About Eve* (1950)
The Hook became *On the Waterfront* (1954)
Tennessee became *Pearl Harbour* (2001)
Diversion became *Fatal Attraction* (1987)
Misled and Uninformed became *Dumb and Dumber* (1994)
Eggs, Beans and Chippendales became *The Full Monty* (1997)

WORDS ON FILM

But *Dumbo* was different. We carried sticky ice cream cones into the large dark room. We each had to sit in our own chair. I had crawled into mine and was turning round peering into the dark where many people sat eating popcorn and candy. My parents were pointing up to a beam of light, and saying 'Dumbo'. I stared at a huge rectangle of light, it was pinkish floating flickering and suddenly I saw... a pig! 'Piglet!' I yelled. 'Piglet was up there! From the book I held on my lap! Piglet who I improved with blue and green crayons was here, huge powerful incandescent unreachable and in motion! I sank into an exquisite passivity staring ahead as dazzling colours flushed and flew, metamorphosing into duck and elephant cat dog house. My parents were happy and proud that I was finally seeing what they saw.

Carolee Schneemann in *Seeing in the Dark:
A Compendium of Cinemagoing*

Bollywood is the nickname for Mumbai (formerly Bombay), the centre of the Indian film industry, which is the most productive film industry in the world. The first film to be made in India was called *Raja Harishchandra* and was made in 1913. Since then more than 67,000 films in more than 30 different languages and dialects have been produced in India. In 2001 alone, 1,013 films came out of the studios of Bollywood, which are mainly family-run. Scripts are written in Hindi or Urdu (or a mix of both), the two main Indian languages which are understood by about 400 million people.

Bollywood movies tend to follow certain formulas and try to appeal to the whole family (these are often known as 'Madras' films, after the popular spice blend that 'has everything in it'). A typical Madras film contains six songs, two exuberant dance scenes, comedy, unconditional love, action, generational conflicts, historical backgrounds, glittery costumes, and a glamorous cast. Due to the number of themes that have to be included, many Bollywood films tend to be much longer than their western counterparts – three hours is not unusual.

Many Bollywood films adapt western narratives and music to Indian tastes, which can lead to extensive borrowing or downright plagiarism. Budgets are far below the Hollywood average, partly due to lower labour costs and partly to the re-use of film sets and costumes. Despite the tight budgets, Bollywood produces epics by the dozen – unlike Hollywood, where epic films are few and far between. Funding in Bollywood is a relatively haphazard business: there are no major studios and until recently, film companies were not eligible for bank loans. Also, there have been several cases of illegitimate funding: in 2001 *Chori Chori Chupke Chupke* had to be withdrawn from cinemas after it emerged that it had been financed by members of the Mumbai underworld.

Bollywood film stars are extremely well paid and are adored by fans. The stars can make or break a film. Some stars make several films at once by jumping between Mumbai film sets.

There are approximately 12,000 cinema screens in India, 13 screens per million head of population. That is the lowest screen average in the world. Over 1,000 multiplexes are to be built in the next few years.

Going to the movies in India is somewhat different from western tradition: the audience comments, applauds, boos and whistles at decisive scenes and it is not uncommon to leave before the end, as soon as the happy ending becomes inevitable.

TRAILER PARK

The movie trailer as we know it today has only been around since the 1960s. Before that trailers told the audience about the film, but that was about it. Trailers were generally cut by the film's editors, almost as an afterthought, to promote the film. They had no budget and were not given much consideration by those making them. By contrast in the twenty-first century, a trailer can make or break a film. The concepts behind trailers have become increasingly complex and they cost about $300,000 to make. Tasters with a minimum of information have become more common, and a well-placed trailer can cause huge anticipation for an upcoming film. When the trailer for *Lord of the Rings: The Fellowship of the Ring* (2001) was released on the internet on 7 April 2001, it was downloaded 1.6 million times in the first 24 hours. The release of a trailer for the second Lord of the Rings film, *The Lord of the Rings: The Two Towers* (2002) shown at the end of the first instalment was enough to make some fans see the film again just to see the trailer, even though the film had been on release for several months and was almost three hours long.

QUOTE UNQUOTE

Although I can accept talking scarecrows, lions and great wizards of emerald cities, I find it hard to believe there is no paperwork involved when your house lands on a witch.
Dave James, writer

BIG SCREEN BEASTIES

Name: Babe

Breed: Large white Yorkshire pig

Film: *Babe* (1995)

Trivia: Shot in Australia, the film had a huge team of 56 animal trainers on set to handle the 970 animals used in the film.

The role of Babe was actually shared by 48 different pigs. The pigs grew too quickly to use just one animal so they were trained in groups of six and used once they reached 15 to 17 weeks old.

Babe's distinguishing feature was a small tuft of black hair on his forehead. This was stuck on to six piglets every day by a make-up artist. Babe's normally white eyelashes were also dyed black to reveal his beautiful eyes.

The film earned seven Oscar nominations and won one for achievement in visual effects.

MIXED-UP MOVIE STARS

Unscramble these famous actors
BIG LEMONS • SCREEN ANNOY
ME MOODIER
Answers on page 153.

BEST SELLING 'BEST SONG' OSCAR WINNING SINGLES IN THE UK

1. **I Just Called To Say I Love You**
Stevie Wonder, *The Woman in Red* (1984)

2. **Fame**
Irene Cara, *Fame* (1980)

3. **Take My Breath Away**
Berlin, *Top Gun* (1986)

4. **My Heart Will Go On**
Celine Dion, *Titanic* (1997)

5. **Flashdance… What A Feeling**
Irene Cara, *Flashdance* (1983)

6. **Evergreen**
Barbra Streisand, *A Star is Born* (1976)

7. **Streets of Philadelphia**
Bruce Springsteen, *Philadelphia* (1994)

8. **Moon River**
Danny Williams, *Breakfast at Tiffany's* (1961)

9. **Whatever Will Be Will Be**
Doris Day, *The Man Who Knew Too Much* (1956)

10. **Raindrops Keep Fallin' On My Head**
Sacha Distel, *Butch Cassidy and the Sundance Kid* (1969)

FIVE STRANGE FILM TITLES

I Killed My Lesbian Wife, Hung Her on a Meat Hook, and Now I Have a Three-Picture Deal at Disney (1993)

SSSSSSS (1973)

Phffft! (1954)

The Film That Rises to the Surface of Clarified Butter (1968)

Don't Worry, We'll Think of a Title (1966)

Speed in mph reached by The Bluesmobile in 1980 film The Blues 115
Brothers *(1980), the speed is real*

WORDS ON FILM

In 1954 I was eight and every Saturday morning I would set off to the movies with my first boyfriend, ten-year-old Skippy. For several hours we would be transported via the newsreel to the exotic East, where American soldiers were valiantly fighting the red, or was it yellow peril, and then to the Wild West, where Hoot Gibson or Eddy Dean would be showing cattle rustlers or unfriendly Indians 'what America stood for'. We would spend the afternoon re-enacting in the parking lot behind the apartment what we had just seen in the morning on the screen. It was then that I began to discover the fate that awaited me as a female. Whilst I saw myself as the hero's faithful sidekick, got up as I was in cowboy gloves with real leather fringes, two guns in holsters buckled on and tied around the leg for the last draw, ten gallon hat and waistcoat, Skippy insisted that I be the daughter of the murdered rancher whose cattle were being rustled. Gradually it began to dawn on me that while in the celluloid world all things were possible, in the other world it was quite a different story.

Marlene Winfield in *Seeing in the Dark:
A Compendium of Cinemagoing*

FADE TO BLACK

**Ten film stars who died while filming and so
never finished their film:**

Jean Harlow, *Saratoga* (1937)
James Dean, *Giant* (1955)
Marilyn Monroe, *Something's Gotta Give* (1962)
Bruce Lee, *Game of Death* (1978)
Natalie Wood, *Brainstorm* (1983)
Vic Morrow, *Twilight Zone: The Movie* (1983)
Brandon Lee, *The Crow* (1994)
River Phoenix, *Dark Blood* (1993)
John Candy, *Wagons East!* (1994)
Oliver Reed, *Gladiator* (2000)

CELEBRITY SELLERS

Not the most expensive items ever sold, but someone wanted them

Marlon Brando's costume from *Mutiny on the Bounty,*
£6,940 in 1997
Jane Seymour's dress from *Live and Let Die*, £2,530 in 1997
Charlton Heston's loin cloth from *Ben Hur*, £6,250 in 1997
Marilyn Monroe's dress from *Some Like it Hot*, £19,800 in 1988
Charlie Chaplin's boots, £38,500 in 1987

The President of the US can enjoy the pleasure of movie-going without leaving home. The 'family theatre' is a part of the residential section of the White House and offers 40 seats set behind four large armchairs with footstools. In 1953, Paul Fischer was appointed the White House projectionist. He kept detailed records of every film that was ever shown at the White House and by whom it was watched, which reveal some fascinating presidential viewing habits.

The film that has been screened the most times in the White House is *High Noon* (1952). Not only was it one of **Dwight Eisenhower's** favourite films, but also **Bill Clinton** said he had seen it more than 20 times. **George W Bush** also watched it soon after the September 11 attacks.

The first film to be watched at the White House was *The Birth of a Nation* (1915) by **Woodrow Wilson**. The film was banned in many cities because of its racist themes and the depiction of the Ku Klux Klan.

Dwight Eisenhower was a fan of westerns and watched over 200 of them. However, he refused to watch any Robert Mitchum film after the actor was convicted of marijuana possession.

JFK did not watch many films because his back problems made sitting in one position for any length of time uncomfortable. However he did watch his favourite actress, Audery Hepburn, in *Roman Holiday* (1953) during the resolution of the Cuban Missile Crisis. In 1960 the president watched *Expresso Bongo* (1960), which starred Cliff Richard. However, it is not known with whom he watched it. The only record from 75 years that is incomplete, simply says that Kennedy had 'one guest'.

Richard Nixon watched *Patton* (1970) in the White House and said it was his favourite film.

Lyndon B Johnson watched one film on a number of occasions; a 10-minute tribute to himself made on the orders of the White House.

Jimmy Carter was the most prolific film watcher and managed 480 screenings in just four years. The first film shown was *All The President's Men* (1976). Despite initially declaring that only family films were to be shown at the White House, he became the first president to watch an X-rated film there: *Midnight Cowboy* (1969).

Ronald Reagan watched very few films but preferred James Stewart films and occasionally watched his own films on special occasions.

Bill Clinton's favourite films were *Schindler's List* (1993) and *American Beauty* (1999).

George W Bush reputedly enjoys the spoof *Austin Powers* series. However he has also watched many war films including *We Were Soldiers* (2002) and *Black Hawk Down* (2001).

FORBIDDEN FILMS

The Last Temptation of Christ (1988) was based on a 1955 novel by Nikos Kazantzakis. The Catholic Church banned the novel and the Greek Orthodox Church excommunicated Kazantzakis.

Christian groups worldwide condemned the film as blasphemous before it was even completed. One thousand two hundred Christian radio stations in California denounced the film, and Christian activist Bill Bright offered to reimburse Universal Studios for its investment in the film in exchange for all existing prints, which he vowed to destroy. Thousands of cinemas refused to screen the film and in 1989, Blockbuster Video decided not to offer it. Despite this public outcry the film's director Martin Scorsese was nominated for a best director Oscar in 1989.

Since January 2002 it has not been permitted for the film to be shown on public television in Bulgaria. The National Television company had scheduled it for showing but the Bulgarian Orthodox Church managed to get an order against it and the Council of Electronic Media banned it.

The television première of the film on Channel 4 in the mid-1990s provoked the greatest number of complaints ever received about a broadcast on British television.

A Catholic group obtained a Supreme Court injunction that has banned the film from cinemas in Chile. If anyone tries to enter the country with a copy of the film, it is confiscated.

THE SOUND OF SUCCESS

Best-selling soundtracks

1.	*The Bodyguard* (1992)	16 times platinum
2.	*Saturday Night Fever* (1977)	15 times
3.	*Purple Rain* (1984)	13 times
4.	*Forrest Gump* (1994)	12 times
5=	*Dirty Dancing* (1987) and *Titanic* (1997)	11 times
7.	*The Lion King* (1994)	10 times
8.	*Top Gun* (1986)	9 times
9=	*Grease* (1978), and *Footloose* (1984)	8 times
11.	*Waiting to Exhale* (1997)	7 times

PUCKER UP

The longest on-screen kiss was between Regis Toomey and Jane Wyman who locked lips for three minutes and five seconds in the 1941 comedy *You're in the Army Now*. At the time, the leading actress Jane Wyman was married to future US president Ronald Reagan.

Mildred wasn't fooled by Cecil's 'begging not to see Dirty Dancing *for the twelfth time' act. She knew that deep down he, too, appreciated Patrick Swayze's genius.*

THE END OF 'THE END'

Once upon a time, far, far away, films ended with a caption simply saying 'The End.' The story of the fate of the caption has been lost in the mists of time but today there is instead an elaborate list of end credits. 'The End' lost favour some time in the 1960s or 1970s and has not been seen since. Stanley Kubrick was one of the few directors to maintain the tradition of the concluding statement and it can be seen at the end of *A Clockwork Orange* (1971).

QUOTE UNQUOTE

Karate is a form of martial arts in which people who have had years and years of training can, using only their hands and feet, make some of the worst movies in the history of the world.
Dave Barry, US humorist

POP BAND FILM FANS

Bad Company (1973, UK) took their name from a Jeff Bridges film *Bad Company* (1972).

Duran Duran (1978, UK) had their first gig at Barbarella's in Birmingham so adopted the name of the character Durand Durand, played by Milo O'Shea in the film *Barbarella* (1968).

Fine Young Cannibals (1984, UK) took their name from the Natalie Wood/Robert Wagner film *All the Fine Young Cannibals* (1960).

Frankie Goes to Hollywood (1980, UK) took their name from a *Variety* magazine headline about Frank Sinatra moving from Las Vegas to Hollywood.

Kajagoogoo (1983, UK) took their name from the original surname of film director Elia Kazan – Kazanjoglou.

Mindbenders (1965, UK) took their name from the Dirk Bogarde film *Mindbenders* (1963).

Roxy Music (1971, UK) named themselves after the Roxy cinema chain.

Searchers (1961, UK) were named after the John Wayne film *The Searchers* (1956).

Ten Thousand Maniacs (1981, US) named themselves after the misheard title of the film, *Two Thousand Maniacs!* (1964).

HAPPY HOUR

Film: *The Thin Man* (1934)

Plot: This detective story features a married couple with a liking for liquor who don't let a small matter of investigating a murder interfere with their drinking schedule. Myrna Loy and William Powell were the tipsy twosome who helped bring the film four Oscar nominations.

Quote: Nick Charles: 'The important thing is the rhythm. Always have rhythm in your shaking. Now a Manhattan you always shake to fox-trot time, a Bronx to two-step time, a dry martini you always shake to waltz time.'

Recipe:
Knickerbocker
50ml gin
Large splash of dry vermouth
Small splash of sweet vermouth

Add the gin and the vermouths to a mixing glass filled with ice. Mix well and strain into a frosted glass.

One day, Carol Reed was directing a scene with Stanley Holloway and some other actors playing a game of darts in my café. He asked me to bustle around in the background, talking Arabic to the extras. I told him that Arabic was one of the enormous quantity of languages I didn't know. He told me to make Arab noises. 'It's almost out of earshot', he said. 'Who's to know?'

I did as I was told, and all went well until take four, when without warning, all the extras rose and left. 'Cut,' said Carol. 'What's wrong?'

They seemed to be on strike, although the reasons for their industrial action were, to say the least, obscure. Eventually it was explained as intermediaries argued with the extras. Apparently, in improvising my Arabic, I had appeared to refer to them as tortoise droppings. I swore to them that nothing had been further from my mind. After all, why should a restaurateur call his clients tortoise droppings while he is taking their orders?

'We thought you didn't speak our language until you called us that unmentionable name,' said the henchman, his eyes flashing with fury. 'Now we know you do!'

Apparently it was not the fact that I had inadvertently referred to them as droppings which was offensive, it was the size of the droppings which counted. Camel droppings, or better, lion droppings, would be deemed almost flattering, as far as insults can be flattering. Flea droppings would have occasioned assault with cutlery. Tortoise droppings were just on the borderline between assault and strike action, and they had taken a clement view of my lapse.

Two hours later, shooting resumed. I steered clear of the tables of the troublemakers, and stuck to Italian.

Peter Ustinov, *Dear Me*

THE KID STAYS IN THE PICTURE

Drew Barrymore (1975–)

'I know certain actors are totally screwed up on drugs, yet it gets covered up. Why wasn't I excused for 'exhaustion' or 'the flu'?'

Barrymore has managed to transform herself firstly from the cute child star of *ET – The Extra Terrestrial* (1982) to the wild child of the late-1980s, with high profile drink and drug problems, to finally becoming a huge Hollywood actress and producer. She is now able to command more than $10 million a film, such as *Charlie's Angels: Full Throttle*, which reportedly netted her a cool $14 million.

---

10 TOP MOVIES

1. *Citizen Kane* (1941)
2. *Casablanca* (1942)
3. *The Godfather* (1972)
4. *Gone with the Wind* (1939)
5. *Lawrence of Arabia* (1962)
6. *The Wizard of Oz* (1939)
7. *The Graduate* (1967)
8. *On the Waterfront* (1954)
9. *Schindler's List* (1993)
10. *Singin' In the Rain* (1952)

As selected by a panel of leaders from across the film community from a list compiled by the American Film Institute in 1998.

10 THINGS LEARNT FROM THE MOVIES

1. All sheets are L-shaped so that after making love the woman will have the sheet up to her shoulders whereas the man will have his chest exposed.
2. All the best detectives get suspended, which is when they invariably solve the case.
3. The only sensible way to investigate strange noises in an unfamiliar house if you are a woman is in skimpy clothing.
4. When foreigners are alone they speak English to each other.
5. Mothers always cook breakfast for their families, who then don't have time to finish them.
6. All single women own a cat.
7. If someone is having a nightmare, they will wake up by sitting bolt upright in bed.
8. All bombs constructed by madmen have a large red display of the time left before they explode.
9. Deciphering the password for a computer system will only take a few attempts.
10. Even if a person is in their mid-twenties, as long as they are stunningly attractive it is possible for them to be a world expert on genetics/nuclear fission/biological warfare.

MOCKUMENTARY OF A ROCKUMENTARY

The term 'rockumentary' is used to describe documentaries about rock stars and their environment and was coined by filmmaker Rob Reiner. Confusingly, it was first used in his film *This is Spinal Tap* (1984), which is a 'mockumentary' – a fiction film presented as a documentary – about a rock band.

WORDS ON FILM

The sign over the box office of the Majestic cinema, Rathby, Leicestershire in the mid 1950s read: 'It's warmer inside'. In summer the word 'warmer' was covered by a wooden panel, hung on the nails, which read 'cooler'. Beneath this, another sign reassured us that 'This cinema is treated with DDT'.

The cinema was built on a hill, giving a natural rake to the auditorium seating. The back two rows of seats, from which every alternate arm rest had been removed, were for 'Couples Only'. At the age of nine I wondered how I would handle my eventual initiation to the back row seating.

...Towards the end of the final reel came the scrape and swish of the velvet curtains being swept across on their metal rods, followed by the clank of the push bars and the sudden rush of cold night air down the back of the neck. A sure signal for those in the 'Couples Only' seats to adjust their dress, and the rest of us to prepare for the pre national anthem stampede. With the crescendo of the closing music the audience scrambled for the exits, leaving national servicemen and isolated royalists standing to attention. It was half a mile to the chip shop, so you had to get a head start.

Chris Garratt in *Seeing in the Dark: A Compendium of Cinemagoing*

FORBIDDEN FILMS

Crash (1996) received strong criticism from the *Daily Mail* and a number of MPs for its immorality. The film, based on JG Ballard's novel, deals with the disturbing sexual relationships between car crash victims. *Crash* generated a considerable amount of controversy even before it was released, and the debate raged in the media about whether it should be shown at all. It was given a release by the BBFC and was banned only by Westminster Council in London.

SOMETHING TO SHOUT ABOUT

In 1951, a scream was recorded for the film *Distant Drums* where it was used in a scene in which a man is bitten and dragged underwater by an alligator. That very same scream has since been used in over 70 films including *The Charge at Feather River* (1953). The character Willhelm screams the famous scream, and since that film the scream has been named after him. The Willhelm Scream has also been used in *Star Wars* (1977), *Raiders of the Lost Ark* (1981), *Poltergeist* (1982), *Beauty and the Beast* (1991), *Batman Returns* (1992), *Reservoir Dogs* (1992), *Toy Story* (1996), *Titanic* (1997) and *The Lord of the Rings: The Two Towers* (2002).

TAGLINE TEASERS

On which movie posters would you see these taglines?

1. A comedy about the greatest love story almost never told.

2. It came for the thrill of the hunt.
   It picked the wrong man.

Answers on page 153.

THE HOLLYWOOD TEN

On 25 November 1947, at the height of the 'Red Scare', a time of intense anti-Communist feeling in the US, a group of 10 American screenwriters and directors suspected to be members of the Communist Party were blacklisted by the major Hollywood studios. The 10 suspects were:

- Herbert J Biberman, writer and director
- Albert Maltz, writer
- Lester Cole, writer
- Dalton Trumbo, writer
- John Howard Lawson, writer
- Alvah Bessie, writer
- Samuel Ornitz, writer
- Ring Lardener Jr, writer
- Edward Dmytryk, director/editor and
- Adrian Scott, writer and producer.

They were fired or suspended indefinitely until an investigation into the allegations raised by the House of Un-American Activities Committee (HUAC) attested to their innocence.

The 'trial' was based on extremely thin evidence, and the committee's interpretation of dialogues and imagery was often far-fetched. Ginger Rogers was one of the famous witnesses and complained that her daughter had been forced to say 'share alike, that's democracy' in *Tender Comrade* (1943), a film written by Dalton Trumbo. The group refused to cooperate with the investigators and eventually two of them were sentenced to six months in prison, the rest to one year. Dalton Trumbo continued to work using a pseudonym (he was involved in writing the script for *Spartacus* (1960)) and Edward Dmytryk was allowed to continue his career after he agreed to testify. But most of the Hollywood Ten had to find another line of work. In the course of the trial many more actors, directors and writers were exposed as 'un-American'. Charlie Chaplin was not allowed to re-enter the US after a trip to Europe and remained abroad until 1972. His film *A King in New York* (1957) satirises the HUAC investigation. Bertolt Brecht, the famous playwright and Nazi refugee, was so disgusted by having to appear in front of a HUAC committee that he emigrated to East Berlin.

MOVIE DOUBLE ACTS

Abbott and Costello

Bud Abbott (1895–1974)
Abbott was the tall, fast-talking straight man of the two.

At Lou Costello's insistence, the monies earned from the 'Abbott and Costello' act were split 60–40, favouring Bud Abbott. Costello stated: 'Comics are a dime a dozen. Good straight men are hard to find.'

Lou Costello (1906–1959)
Costello was the short, chubby funny man.

He had only one starring role in a feature film without Bud Abbott, *The 30 Foot Bride of Candy Rock* (1959). He died before it was released.

They made 36 films together, including their *Abbott and Costello Meet...* series:

Bud Abbott Lou Costello Meet Frankenstein (1948)
Abbott and Costello Meet the Killer, Boris Karloff (1949)
Abbott and Costello Meet the Invisible Man (1951)
Abbott and Costello Meet Captain Kidd (1952)
Abbott and Costello Meet Dr. Jekyll and Mr. Hyde (1953)
Abbott and Costello Meet the Mummy (1955)
Abbott and Costello Meet the Keystone Kops (1955)

WORDS ON FILM

'Everything ready?' said Dr. Brodsky in a very breathy goloss. Then I could hear slooshy voices saying Right right right from like a distance, then nearer to, then there was a quiet humming shoom as though things had been switched on. And then the lights went out and there was Your Humble Narrator And Friend sitting alone in the dark, all on his frightened oddy knocky, not able to move nor shut his galzzies nor anything. And then, O my brothers, the film-show started off with some very gromky atmosphere music coming from the speakers, very fierce and full of discord. And then on the screen the picture came on, but there was no title and no credits. What came on was a street, as it might have been any street in any town, and it was real dark nochy and the lamps were lit. it was a very good like professional piece of sinny, and there were none of these flickers and blobs you get, say, when you viddy one of these dirty films in somebody's house in a back street.

Anthony Burgess,
A Clockwork Orange

I'M YOUR BIGGEST FAN

Mickey Mouse was reported to have received 800,000 fan letters in 1933, an average of 66,000 a month. The small technicality that he's not real did little to deter the hoards of Disney devotees. Chasing the revered rodent in the fan mail stakes was child star Shirley Temple who received an average of 60,000 letters a month in her 1936 heyday. Charlie Chaplin received 73,000 letters in just three days in 1921, and Clara Bow received 33,727 items of mail during April of 1928. The cost of replying was $2,550, including $450 for three full-time secretaries.

10 GREATEST VILLAINS

Dr Hannibal Lecter (*The Silence of the Lambs*, 1991)
Norman Bates (*Psycho*, 1960)
Darth Vader (*The Empire Strikes Back*, 1980)
The Wicked Witch of the West (*The Wizard of Oz*, 1939)
Nurse Ratched (*One Flew Over the Cuckoo's Nest*, 1975)
Mr Potter (*It's a Wonderful Life*, 1946)
Alex Forrest (*Fatal Attraction*, 1987)
Phyllis Dietrichson (*Double Indemnity*, 1944)
Regan MacNeil (*The Exorcist*, 1973)
The Queen (*Snow White and the Seven Dwarfs*, 1937)

In a ballot held by the American Film Institute in 2003 the greatest villains were selected by a panel of distinguished members of the film community, from directors, screenwriters, actors, editors, cinematographers, visual effects artists, stunt men and women and make-up artists.

THEY SHOULD HAVE STAYED AT HOME

Pee-wee Herman (1952–)

American actor and comedian Paul Reubens is best known for the character Pee-wee Herman, an infantile man with slick, short hair and a grey suit worn a size too small. He starred in various films throughout the 80s including his most famous role in the family comedy *Pee-wee's Big Adventure* (1985). In 1991, his image as a children's entertainer was dealt a big blow when he was arrested in an 'adult' cinema for masturbating in public. The actor had been visiting his parents in Sarasota, Florida and went out to see the X-rated film *Nancy Nurse*. He was arrested, although later released on bail. The media soon heard of the story and his career as a family entertainer was seriously affected. His television show *The Pee-wee Herman Show* had already finished airing but re-runs were cancelled indefinitely. Reubens now lives a reclusive life in Los Angeles doing occasional film and television work.

When artistic vision is forced to compete with capital gain, in Hollywood there is only ever one winner. Each new film receives a test screening, at which the audience passes comment, and the film may then be edited accordingly. So, when a test audience reacted negatively to the original ending of *Fatal Attraction* (1987) – Glenn Close's character committed suicide and Michael Douglas was arrested for her murder – actors were recalled, scenes were re-shot and the rest is cinematic history.

However, it's not just test audiences who have been known to meddle with endings; actors, writers, editors and executives have all rewritten final scenes over the years.

Blade Runner (1982)
Beset with conflict between the director, the editors and the film studio, *Blade Runner* is now available to watch in at least three different versions (none of which Ridley Scott is said to be truly happy with). Even before these problems, however, Ridley Scott was in two minds concerning how the film should end – his original vision hinted that Harrison Ford's character was in fact a replicant.

Back To The Future (1985)
Following its critical and box office success, and the subsequent commissioning of two sequels, when *BTTF* was prepared for VHS release the studio tacked an imposing 'To be continued...' title between the final scene and the closing credits. They made two

more films, and we *never* questioned their motives.

28 Days Later (2002)
Unsure as to how to end their viral-zombie flick, director Danny Boyle and writer Alex Garland, wrote and recorded two endings. The first brimmed with Hollywood optimism and the second was significantly bleaker. The former was selected for the UK cinematic release but, in the spirit of consumer choice, the US cinemas screened both.

Clue (1985)
Three endings were shot and shown at random cinemas. In each ending a different guest was the murderer. All three versions were included on the DVD and video.

NOT ON OUR SCREENS

They all failed screen tests:
Fred Astaire • Tallulah Bankhead
Brigitte Bardot • Maurice Chevalier
Clark Gable • Cary Grant
Robert de Niro • Laurence Olivier
Jane Russell • Shirley Temple

Number of takes Stanley Kubrick demanded from Shelley Duvall for one 127
scene in The Shining *(1980)*

A Hard Day's Night (1964)
Mockumentary about a 'typical' day with the Beatles at the height of Beatlemania. The film follows the group into hotel rooms, TV studios and backstage areas. Interestingly, the word 'Beatles' is never mentioned in the movie.

Glitter (2001)
Loosely based on Mariah Carey's life story. The film was a box office flop and Mariah received two Razzie awards: one for worst actress and one for worst screen couple (for her cleavage).

Spiceworld (1997)
The Spice Girls on tour. Frank Bruno was supposed to assume a key cameo role, but pulled out after a 'disagreement with major cast members'. In the end, Meatloaf played his part. All band members won a worst actress Razzie award.

Crossroads (2002)
Britney Spears plays an aspiring singer, who goes on a road trip to LA to attend an audition. She falls in love with cute guy Ben (Anson Mount), who reputedly agreed to play the part only because Robert De Niro encouraged him to do so. De Niro even helped Mount by going over scenes with him – Mount reading Ben's and De Niro reading Britney's bits.

Leningrad Cowboys Go America (1991)
Cult film about Siberian rock band Leningrad Cowboys trying to make it in the USA. The members of the 'worst rock band in the world' are known for their trademark enormous quiffs and extremely pointy cowboy boots.

200 Motels (1971)
Twisted fantasy/comedy featuring Frank Zappa and The Mothers of Invention. After bassist Jeff Simmons quit the band, Zappa decided to give his role to the next person who entered London's Pinewood studios, where the film was being made – it was Ringo Starr's chauffeur.

8 Mile (2002)
Rapper Eminem's screen debut received a warm welcome from the critics and 'Lose Yourself' won an Academy award for best original song.

Bodyguard (1992)
Whitney Houston plays a pop star having to deal with fame, stalkers and a good-looking bodyguard (Kevin Costner). The idea for the film first came up in the mid-1970s, Diana Ross was supposed to play the leading role but the project fell through because it was 'too controversial'.

Loving You (1957)
The first of several films in which Elvis Presley plays a rock 'n' roll singer on the way to or struggling with stardom. *Roustabout* (1964); *Spinout* (1966) and *Double Trouble* (1967) followed.

THE REVISED SCRIPT WAS BETTER

Frankly my dear, I don't give a ham.

TOP 10 FILM BUDGETS

Film	Year	Budget ($)
Titanic	1997	200,000,000
Waterworld	1995	175,000,000
Wild Wild West	1999	175,000,000
Terminator 3: Rise of the Machines	2003	170,000,000
Van Helsing	2004	170,000,000
Troy	2004	150,000,000
Tarzan	1999	145,000,000
Die Another Day	2002	142,000,000
Armageddon	1998	140,000,000
Lethal Weapon 4	1998	140,000,000
Men in Black II	2002	140,000,000
Pearl Harbour	2001	140,000,000
Treasure Planet	2002	140,000,000

QUOTE UNQUOTE

Of all the potential problems facing our planet, a hurtling asteroid is probably the one in which our store of information is most completely dependent on bad movies.
New York Times, *13 March 1998*

Number of identifiable foreign countries Hollywood films were set in 129
between 1912 and 1999

Spring gave way, rather grudgingly, I thought, to summer and in late June we were about to complete the last shot of the film. It was an uncomfortable shot that was almost lethal for me. A replica of the bridge of the destroyer had been made out of light wood and real glass and placed on the edge of the large outside tank at Denwood Studios. Above it, a few hundred yards away on a scaffolding, were perched two enormous tanks filled with thousands of gallons of water. On a given signal a lever would be pulled, whereupon the tanks would disgorge their load down a chute, and overturn and capsize the bridge with me on it. Shivering in the bitter summer weather, I looked at the flimsy structure on which I was to stand and then up at the tanks and said 'No.' David and Ronnie, whose nonchalant attitude to human endurance had been engendered by years of film making, looked at me with rather contemptuous disappointment. If I was frightened, David said, a stand-in would do it first, although this would entail a three hours' wait while the tanks were filled up again. These words, obviously intended as a spur to my failing courage, fell on stony ground for the simple reason that I knew a great deal more about the weight of water than they did. I replied that in no circumstances would I either do it myself or allow any living creature to stand on the bridge until I saw what the impact of water would do to it. Finally, after some grumbling at the time waste, they gave in to my insistence and ordered the signal to be given. The whistle blew and we all stood back and watched. There was a loud roar as the released water came hurtling down the chute and, in a split second, there was nothing left of the bridge at all. It was immediately obvious to all concerned that anyone standing on it would have been killed instantly. David and Ronnie, pale and trembling, returned silently with me to my dressing-room, where we each of us drowned a strong tot of brandy.

Noel Coward, *Autobiography*

CAMEO

Although the term 'cameo' has existed long before films were invented, the term 'cameo role' was first coined in the 1950s. The film *Around the World in Eighty Days* (1956) featured at least 44 credited appearances by famous people in small parts. Cameo consequently came to mean a small part played by a famous person. Some of the people who made appearances in Michael Anderson's film include:

Buster Keaton • Noel Coward
Frank Sinatra • John Gielgud
Marlene Dietrich

THE CRITICAL LIST

Barry Norman (1933–)

Norman was the leading light of BBC film reviewing for 26 years and the anchor of *Film '72*, which he presented until it became *Film '99*, when he handed over to Jonathan Ross. He began his career as a journalist on the *Kensington News* and worked on the *Daily Mail* as showbiz editor. He was also a writer of the 'Flook' comic strip cartoon in the *Daily Mail*.

He maintains that he never said his supposed catchphrase 'And why not?', which was bestowed on him by impressionist Rory Bremner on Bremner's television show. But the phrase stuck so firmly that people strongly believe that Norman has been using it for decades, and to prove he has a sense of humour, he used it for the title of his autobiography.

From his book *100 Best Films of the Century* (1992) his list of favourites can be broken down into decades as follows:

Decade	Number of Films
20s	4
30s	19
40s	26
50s	24
60s	7
70s	11
80s	5
90s	4

QUOTE UNQUOTE

If I made Cinderella, the audience would be looking out for a body in the coach.
Alfred Hitchcock, US film director

TOP 10 CINEMA-GOING COUNTRIES

Country	Average admissions per capita
USA	5.58
Iceland	5.54
Australia	5.05
Singapore	4.72
Ireland	4.36
New Zealand	4.23
Canada	3.99
Spain	3.74
Luxembourg	3.35
Hong Kong	3.30

Right in the middle of the death scene in Love Story,
*Geoff suddenly found that his 3-D glasses were also equipped
with Tickle-around.*

DON'T YOU FORGET ABOUT ME

The National Film Registry in the US preserves films of cultural merit and holds a copy of them in the library of Congress in Washington DC. Films need to be preserved because film decays within years if not properly stored as it is made of perishable plastic. The Library of Congress has documented that fewer than 20% of US feature films from the 1920s survive intact in American archives. Today, with better technology and the advent of television, VHS and DVD, films live on long after their original release. However, to combat the problem of lost films the National Film Registry has started to save films. Every year 25 films are deemed worthy to be preserved. Public nominations are accepted for films but must meet the following criteria:

1. They must be culturally, historically, or aesthetically significant

2. They must be at least 10 years old

The work started in 1989 and over 300 films have already been deemed worthy of preservation. The earliest films to be saved are both from 1896 and are *Rip Van Winkle*, preserved in 1995 and *The Kiss*, preserved in 1999.

Making a new master and viewing print of a black-and-white seven-reel silent feature costs about $32,000, assuming that no special restoration is needed.

Couple: Angelina Jolie and Billy Bob Thornton
Film: *Pushing Tin* (1999)
Love story: This normal-as-they-come couple met while playing a married couple in *Pushing Tin* and married in early 2000. At the time Thornton was dating actress Laura Dern who has said: 'I left our home to work on a movie, and while I was away, my boyfriend got married, and I've never heard from him again.' They got married wearing vials of each other's blood around their necks. Thornton had already been married four times and Jolie once. They have since divorced.

Couple: Elizabeth Taylor and Richard Burton
Film: *Cleopatra* (1963)
Love story: Within weeks of arriving on the set of *Cleopatra*, Taylor and Burton had started an affair. They were both married at the time but divorced their respective spouses so they could tie their own knot in 1964. They became the most famous married couple in the world and went on to star in seven films together in five years before divorcing in 1974. They then re-married in 1975 for less than a year.

Couple: Goldie Hawn and Kurt Russell
Film: *Overboard* (1987)
Love story: The couple have never actually married but have been together for over 15 years and have a child together. Goldie's actress daughter from a previous marriage, Kate Hudson, calls Kurt 'Dad.'

MOVIE STARS AND THEIR INITIALS

WC Fields – William Claude
Samuel L Jackson – Leroy
William H Macy – Hall
M Night Shyamalan – Manoj
John C Reilly – Christopher
DW Griffith – David Wark
Richard E Grant – Esterhuysen
F Murray Abraham – Fahrid
Edward G Robinson – Goldberg
Lee J Cobb – Jacoby
P T Anderson – Paul Thomas
Michael J Fox – the J doesn't actually stand for anything, as his real middle name is Andrew. Michael adopted the J as homage to the character actor Michael J Pollard.

Lights, camera, action, special effects, CGI... none of these is found in a Dogme 95 film and neither are editing, props, make-up or neatly written musical scores. The Dogme 95 collective of film directors was founded in 1995 in Copenhagen, to counteract modern tendencies in film making. Although the first four Dogme films were Danish-produced and directed, directors from Argentina to Korea, and the US have since joined in. Their goal is to remove all technological illusions and distractions, and go back to basics 'in search of the truth'.

The first ever Dogme film was *Festen* (1998), directed by Thomas Vinterberg. Other directors involved in the founding wave of the movement include Lars von Trier, director of *Dancer in the Dark* (2000) and Søren Kragh-Jacobsen, director of *Mifune's Last Song* (1999).

Directors must accept the following Vow of Chastity:

'I swear to submit to the following set of rules drawn up and confirmed by Dogme 95:

1. Shooting must be done on location. Props and sets must not be brought in. (If a particular prop is necessary for the story, a location must be chosen where this prop is to be found.)
2. The sound must never be produced apart from the images or vice versa. (Music must not be used unless it occurs where the scene is being shot.)
3. The camera must be hand-held. Any movement or immobility attainable in the hand is permitted. (The film must not take place where the camera is standing; shooting must take place where the film takes place.)
4. The film must be in colour. Special lighting is not acceptable. (If there is too little light for exposure the scene must be cut or a single lamp be attached to the camera.)
5. Optical work and filters are forbidden.
6. The film must not contain superficial action. (Murders, weapons, etc must not occur.)
7. Temporal and geographical alienation are forbidden. (That is to say that the film takes place here and now.)
8. Genre movies are not acceptable.
9. The film format must be Academy 35mm.
10. The director must not be credited.

I also swear to refrain from personal taste and to refrain from creating a 'work', as I regard the instant as more important than the whole. My supreme goal is to force the truth out of my characters and settings. I swear to do so by all the means available and at the cost of any good taste and any aesthetic considerations.

Thus I make my VOW OF CHASTITY.'

134 *Weight, in carats, of the diamonds in the necklace worn by Nicole Kidman in* Moulin Rouge *(2001)*

10 MOST THRILLING FILMS

1. *Psycho* (1960)
2. *Jaws* (1975)
3. *The Exorcist* (1973)
4. *North by Northwest* (1959)
5. *The Silence of the Lambs* (1991)
6. *Alien* (1979)
7. *The Birds* (1963)
8. *The French Connection* (1971)
9. *Rosemary's Baby* (1968)
10. *Raiders of the Lost Ark* (1981)

In a ballot held by the American Film Institute in 2001 the most thrilling films were selected by a panel of distinguished members of the film community, from directors, screenwriters, actors, editors, cinematographers, visual effects artists, stunt men and women and make-up artists.

WORDS ON FILM

A refurbished *Star Wars* is on somewhere or everywhere. I have no intention of revisiting any galaxy. I shrivel inside each time it is mentioned. Twenty years ago, when the film was first shown, it had a freshness, also a sense of moral good and fun. Then I began to be uneasy at the influence it might be having. The bad penny first dropped in San Francisco when a sweet-faced boy of twelve told me proudly that he had seen *Star Wars* over a hundred times. His elegant mother nodded with approval. Looking into the boy's eyes I thought I detected little star-shells of madness beginning to form and I guessed that one day they would explode.

'I would love you to do something for me,' I said

'Anything! Anything!' the boy said rapturously.

'You won't like what I'm going to ask you to do,' I said.

'Anything, sir, anything!'

'Well,' I said, 'do you think you could promise never to see *Star Wars* again?'

He burst into tears. His mother drew herself up to an immense height. 'What a *dreadful* thing to say to a child!' she barked, and dragged the poor kid away. Maybe she was right but I just hope the lad, now in his thirties, is not living in a fantasy world of second-hand, childish banalities.

Alec Guinness, A Positively Final Appearance

NOT SO FUNNY FOREIGNERS

In 1998, a *New York Times* article appeared listing film titles that had been 'hilariously' translated into various languages in Asia. The writer James Sterngold offered the following examples:

Leaving Las Vegas (1995):	'I'm Drunk and You Are a Prostitute' (Hong Kong)
The Crying Game (1992):	'Oh No! My Girlfriend Has a Penis!' (Hong Kong)
Barb Wire (1996):	'Delicate Orbs of Womanhood Bigger Than Your Head Can Hurt You' (China)
George of the Jungle (1997):	'Big Dumb Monkey Man Keep Whacking Tree with Genitals' (China)

These 'so-funny-you-couldn't-make-it-up' titles were in fact... made up. The journalist subsequently admitted having found the information online and had not checked his sources. It later emerged that they had come from a spoof website. Although all seem frighteningly plausible.

QUOTE UNQUOTE

No matter how sheltered and virginal the heroine, at the moment of crisis, it turns out that she has all along been an expert kick-boxer.
David Frum, US writer, on *Pirates of the Caribbean: The Curse of the Black Pearl* (2003)

LITTLE IN BRITAIN TO BIG IN HOLLYWOOD

Although there are many British stars in Hollywood, there are many more who crossed the Atlantic only to sink without trace. However, it seems that one way to help your chances is by getting a small part in a British drama or soap. Television producers looking through their past cast lists have found some rather big names who once played rather small parts.

Casualty – Helen Baxendale, Orlando Bloom, Minnie Driver, Christopher Eccleston, Brenda Fricker, Jonny Lee Miller, Parminder Nagra, Kate Winslet

The Bill – Sean Bean, Paul Bettany, John Hannah, Alex Kingston, Keira Knightly

Coronation Street – Davy Jones, Ben Kingsley, Joanne Whalley

Eastenders – Martine McCutcheon

MIXED-UP MOVIE STARS

Unscramble theses famous actors
HANG THEN BANKER • RISK BIG NAME
COAL PAIN
Answer on page 153.

WORST CINEMA DISASTERS

Country (date)	Incident	No. killed
1. China (18/02/1977)	Cinema fire	694
2. China (13/02/1937)	Cinema fire	658
3. Iran (22/08/1978)	Cinema fire (arson by extremists)	422
4. China (08/12/1994)	Cinema fire	324
5. Syria (13/11/1960)	Cinema fire/stampede	152
6. Puerto Rico (20/06/1919)	Cinema fire/panic	150
7. Russia (12/03/1929)	Cinema fire	150
8. China (20/05/1930)	Cinema fire	130
9. South Korea (10/05/1930)	Cinema fire and panic	104
10. Turkey (21/09/1924)	Cinema fire	104

BOND TRAVELS

Mr Bond has travelled the world over during his 40 odd years of service, and while Bond films can expect to do well across the world, the films often take on slightly confusing titles when translated. In a kind of international game of Chinese whispers, here are some examples of Bond film titles when translated into another language and then back again:

Dr. No (1962)
Spain: 'Agent 007 vs. The Satanic Dr. No'

From Russia With Love (1963)
Germany: 'Love Greetings From Moscow'

You Only Live Twice (1967)
Japan: '007 Dies Twice'

On Her Majesty's Secret Service (1969)
China: '007 Seized the Snow Mountain Castle'

Moonraker (1979)
China: '007 Seized the Space Complex'

The Living Daylights (1987)
Greece: 'With the Finger in the Trigger'

Some Famous Misquotations

'Me Tarzan, you Jane' is often inaccurately quoted from *Tarzan, the Ape Man* (1932) The actual lines were:

Jane: (pointing to herself) Jane.
Tarzan: (he points at her) Jane.
Jane: And you? (she points at him) You?
Tarzan: (stabbing himself proudly in the chest) Tarzan, Tarzan.
Jane: (emphasising his correct response) Tarzan.
Tarzan: (poking back and forth each time) Jane. Tarzan. Jane. Tarzan...

'Play it again, Sam' was never spoken by Ingrid Bergman or Humphrey Bogart in *Casablanca* (1942) to Sam (Dooley Wilson), the nightclub pianist and reluctant performer of the song 'As Time Goes By' (written by Herman Hupfeld). Variations on the line were spoken, however, by the two leads:

Rick says: You played it for her, you can play it for me. Play it!'
Ilsa says: Play it, Sam. Play 'As Time Goes By'.
The line 'Play it again, Sam' appears in the Marx Brothers' *A Night in Casablanca* (1946).

'We have ways of making you talk' was never actually in the film *Lives of a Bengal Lancer* (1935). The actual line was: 'We have ways of making men talk' and was spoken by Douglass Dumbrille.

The mobster soundbite, 'You dirty rat!' was never said verbatim by James Cagney, although he did say something similar: 'Mmm, that dirty, double-crossin' rat,' in *Blonde Crazy* (1931). In *Home Alone* (1990), Macauley Culkin watched a scene from a fictional black and white gangster film videotape titled *Angels With Filthy Souls* (a take-off on the Cagney film *Angels With Dirty Faces* (1938), in which a gangster shoots his girlfriend, while saying, 'Take that, you dirty rat!'

'If you build it, they will come' was not what the voice said in *Field of Dreams* (1989). Instead, it was: 'If you build it, he will come.' In *Wayne's World 2* (1993) there is a reference to the line where Wayne says 'If we book them, they will come.'

One of the most oft-quoted lines in cinema history has often been misquoted. 'Badges? We don't need no stinkin' badges!' in *The Treasure of the Sierra Madre* (1948) was actually: 'Badges? We ain't got no badges. We don't need no badges. I don't have to show you any stinkin' badges!'

QUOTE UNQUOTE

Nobody should come to the movies unless he believe in heroes
John Wayne, US actor

138 *Number of the car registration plate on John Milner's car in* American Graffiti (1973), *THX-138.*

MOST SUCCESSFUL INDIAN FILMS
SHOWN IN THE UK

Film	Year	UK Total (£)
1. *Kabhi Khushi Kabhi Gham*	2001	2,222,898
2. *Monsoon Wedding*	2001	2,104,439
3. *Devdas*	2002	1,663,692
4. *Hum Aapke Hai Kaun*	1994	1,530,000
5. *Dilwale Dulhaniya Le Jayenge*	1995	1,490,000
6. *Kuch Kuch Hota Hai*	1998	1,441,000
7. *Mohabbatein*	2000	1,100,000
8. *Lagaan*	2001	681,521
9. *Hum Tumhare Hain Sanam*	2002	663,778
10. *Mujhse Dosti Karoge*	2002	611,164

SAINTLY CINEMA

While there seems to be no evidence of the cinema having its own patron saint, those who practice the Catholic faith do have a wide web of support open to them. When deciding which film to see they might call upon Saint Expeditus, the patron saint of procrastination, which should be followed swiftly by a prayer to Saint Angela of Foligno – one of the many saints that help to fight temptation – as soon as they reach the popcorn counter.

Once the film has started, help might be sought from Saints Blaise, Quentin and Walburga (against coughs), Saint Ursicinus of Saint-Ursanne (against a stiff neck), Saints Cornelius and Polycarp of Smyrna (against earache) and, if worst comes to worst, Saint Bonaventure (against bowel disorders).

Although unable to guarantee his intervention, it also might be worth remembering Saint Dominic Savio, the patron saint assigned to the protection (and, we can only hope, the control) of juvenile delinquents.

As might be expected, should any of the actors (protected by Saints Genesius of Rome, Vitus or Pelagia the penitent) get a little raunchy, Saints Catherine of Siena, Margaret of Cortona, Mary of Edessa, Mary of Egypt, Mary Magdalen of Pazzi and Pelagia of Antioch, can be appealed to provide strength in the face of sexual temptation.

Finally, as the evening draws to a close and the inevitable coat pocket rummaging reveals that they were your keys that clattered to the carpet when the entire row stood to receive the late-comer, who are you going to call? Catholics would call on Saint Zita... before quickly calling the Multiplex of course.

Number of films between 1910 and 2000 made on the theme of 139
horse racing

As I took my place with two jamjars in my first Saturday morning kids matinee queue, apprehensive lest the currency had been devalued or even replaced with money, I observed that not only were Royals the heroes in the films but that my choice of cinema was between the Queens and the Royal, and I was warned that before the performance you were supposed to stand for the pianist's rendition of 'God save the King'. I took against this practice and reflected later that 'God save the People of Wallsend' would have been more appropriate, for few in authority cared much, let alone had the power to assuage the people's meagre needs...

I want you to recall with me Chaplin in *City Lights*. Charlie has taken a street sweeper's job to earn the money to pay off the cruel landlord who would otherwise put a blind girl and her mother out onto the streets. It was like that in Wallsend in those days. In addition Charlie needs to raise enough money to finance an operation to restore the girl's sight. No money, no sight: that was the way it was before the National Health Service came to Wallsend. Imagine Charlie with his sweeping brush and shovel neatly disposing of a pile of horse droppings and then, looking into the camera, observing a passing elephant. A twitch of his moustache, a movement of the eyebrow, and what else did he need to do? When the new sighted flower girl sees not a handsome, well groomed, six foot Adonis her eyes reveal something different. You see *he was a hero*, a social hero, a small guy, a fall guy, not necessarily a brave or courageous guy, usually the opposite. Chaplin was telling me that such people don't qualify for medals or monuments, unlike those who fight and kill or wound, or are killed or wounded.

I was and remain a supporter of Chaplin's view.

T Dan Smith in
Seeing in the Dark: A Compendium of Cinemagoing

LOCATION...NOT WHERE YOU'D EXPECT

Place and Film	Location
Middle Earth in *The Lord of the Rings* (2001–2003)	New Zealand
Tatooine in *Star Wars* (1977)	Tunisia
Mars in *Red Planet* (2000)	Australia and Jordan
Jamaica in *Cool Runnings* (1993)	Canada
North Carolina in *Cold Mountain* (2003)	Romania
America in *The Good, The Bad and The Ugly* (1966)	Spain
Scotland in *Braveheart* (1995)	Ireland
Mystery barren planet in *Pitch Black* (2000)	Australia
Vietnam in *Full Metal Jacket* (1987)	England

MGM

Logo: a roaring lion and the motto *Ars Gratia Artis* (Art for Art's Sake).

In 1924 the merger of Metro Picture Organisation, Goldwyn Picture Corporation and Louis B Mayer Pictures led to the formation of Metro Goldwyn Mayer Pictures. During the 1930s, MGM was the market leader, and produced blockbusters such as *Tarzan* (1934), *Grand Hotel* (1932), *Gone with the Wind* (1939) and *The Wizard of Oz* (1939). After World War Two, MGM focused on musicals and had Fred Astaire, Gene Kelly and Frank Sinatra under contract. In the late 1950s, the studio started making losses, despite hits like *Ben Hur* (1959) and re-releasing older films. In 1969, the studio was bought (some say raided) by Kirk Kerkorian who began dismantling its film production units and building up an extensive back catalogue of films by buying up other companies' archives. In 1979, MGM announced that it would focus on its hotel business, although it has since produced a few successful films, including the James Bond series (1962–2002) and *Legally Blonde* (2001).

KING OF THE CASTLE

William Castle (1914–1977) was a prolific B-movie director throughout the 1940s, 1950s and 1960s. Although he never received acclaim as a director, he secured his place in movie-going memory by creating his own brand of film hype. A great believer in the power of hype, he used unusual gimmicks to sell tickets which included:

- Castle took out an insurance policy against 'death by fright' with Lloyds of London for *Macabre* (1958). During its first cinematic release, the audience members were given a small badge that said 'I'm no chicken. I saw *Macabre*.'
- At certain key moments in the showings of *House on Haunted Hill* (1959), a glow-in-the-dark skeleton appeared from the screen and swooped over the heads of the audience.
- Whenever there were screams in *The Tingler* (1959), hidden buzzers would vibrate the seats of the audience. Castle also installed fake audience members who would let out screams at scripted times.
- In *13 Ghosts* (1960), the audience were given special glasses to view the ghosts on the screen as the film had been filmed in 'Illusion-O.'
- There was a one-minute 'fright break' in *Homicidal* (1961) so that audience members who were faint of heart could leave the cinema.
- Audiences were given luminous thumbs for *Mr Sardonicus* (1961) with which to vote thumbs-up or thumbs-down. The audience voted on whether the main character could live or die, even though Castle shot only one ending for the film.

Critics were divided over the cultural adjustments made to the Dutch remake of Attack of the 50 Foot Woman.

COUNTRIES THAT PRODUCED THE
MOST FILMS IN THE 1990S

1. India	839
2. China and Hong Kong SAR	469
3. Philippines	456
4. USA	385
5. Japan	238

The UK came in 11th with 78 films.

Nine countries that did not produce any films in the 1990s:
Bahamas • Bahrain
Benin • Cambodia
Chad • Kenya
Namibia • Nicaragua
Rwanda

Oscars

Why are Academy Awards called Oscars?
There is no definitive answer but the most credible theory is that an Academy librarian, on seeing the statue for the first time, said it reminded her of her Uncle Oscar. A journalist overheard her and so the nickname stuck. The name was used officially for the first time in 1939.

At the first awards in 1929, the winners were already known and had been printed in a late edition of newspapers. Sealed envelopes were introduced in 1930.

The Godfather Part II (1974) is the only sequel to have won best picture.

Gone with the Wind (1939) is the longest film to have won best picture at a whopping three hours and 42 minutes.

Marty (1955) is the shortest film to have won best picture at just 91 minutes.

Around the World in Eighty Days (1956) and *One Flew Over the Cuckoo's Nest* (1975) have the longest titles of all best picture winners. The shortest title of a best picture winner is *Gigi* (1958).

Three films that have won every award they were nominated for:
Gigi (1958): 9 awards
The Last Emperor (1987): 9 awards
The Lord of the Rings: The Return of the King (2003): 11 awards

Two films that were nominated for 11 awards but did not win any:
The Turning Point (1977)
The Color Purple (1985)

Anthony Quinn was on screen for only eight minutes in *Lust for Life* (1956) but he managed to scoop the best supporting actor award.

Shirley Temple is the youngest person to receive an award. She was presented with a juvenile Academy Award at the age of six years and 310 days. The youngest winner of an Oscar in a competitive category was Tatum O'Neal, who at the age of 10 years and 148 days won a supporting actress Oscar for *Paper Moon* (1973).

TAGLINE TEASERS

On which movie posters would you see these taglines?

1. Let's go to work.

2. On the air. Unaware.

Answers on page 153.

Joan Crawford (1904–1977) and Bette Davis (1908–1989)

'Why am I so good at playing bitches? I think it's because I'm not a bitch. Maybe that's why Miss Crawford always plays ladies.' *Bette Davis*

'Bette will play anything, as long as she thinks someone is watching... I'm a little more selective than that.' *Joan Crawford*

No one really knows when the rivalry between Crawford and Davis started; although it was said that Bette had an affair with her co-star Franchot Tone in the 1935 film *Dangerous* who became Crawford's husband soon after the film wrapped. The pair did not cross professionally until they were both at Warner Brothers studios in the 1940s. At first Bette was the bigger star and had first choice of all roles, but by the mid 1940s she was starting to slip. When she overlooked the lead in *Mildred Pierce* (1945) for which Joan won the best actress Oscar, Bette was less than happy about being eclipsed.

However, Davis managed to trump Joan by playing the lead in *The Star* (1952), a film about a has-been actress who was a thinly disguised portrayal of Joan. The script was written by Crawford's disgruntled former friends. Need-less to say, Joan despised Bette for her part in this humiliation. In 1952 both actresses were up for best actress, Joan for *Sudden Fear* and Bette for *The Star*. Neither won, but the feud continued.

Both their careers were consigned to co-star roles until 1962 when they were given the joint leads in *Whatever Happened To Baby Jane?* Bette demanded top billing and more money but Joan made sure that their names were given equal billing. The press were desperate for the feud to erupt but the women denied there was any ill feeling, as both were aware of how important this film was for their careers. However, Joan, who was the widow of the president of Pepsi Cola, posed for photographs with Pepsi and inundated the set with the product. Bette retaliated by posing for Coca-Cola photographs. Both actresses wanted an Oscar nomination but only Bette received one. However, Joan was not to be outdone and offered to accept the award on behalf of any of the actresses who could not be there on the night. When Anne Bancroft won, Joan took to the stage and spent the rest of the night with the winners. The feud simmered on until the late 1970s when Joan died in 1977.

QUOTE UNQUOTE

If my films make one more person miserable,
I'll feel I have done my job.
Woody Allen, US filmmaker

HAPPY HOUR

Film: *The Philadelphia Story* (1940)

Plot: Socialite Tracey Lord is about to marry for the second time. Unfortunately her ex-husband shows up with two tabloid journalists the day before the wedding, determined to ruin it. The bride is somewhat perturbed but not enough to interrupt some monumental drinking sessions.

Quote: Macaulay Connor: 'I would sell my grandmother for a drink – and you know how I love my grandmother.'

Recipe:
Kir Royale
10ml crème de cassis
dry champagne
Fill a champagne flute three quarters full with the champagne. Then add the crème de cassis and garnish with a twist of lemon.

WORDS ON FILM

Cinema was not just an entertainment for our generation. It was a medicine, an antidote to the monstrous reality outdoors. Films reflected another world, where comfort, joy and love were possible. Movies were life and reality, and what happened in the murderous streets an absurd nightmare.

Censorship, dictated by the military and Catholic priests, cut a lot. Dubbing films became obligatory by law, and they took advantage of it to change the dialogue. In their anxiety to eliminate sinful love they presented lovers as relatives, thus transforming the boring Hollywood sex code into a frolic of perversions. We could see Garbo kissing her father in a most peculiar way, and Ava Gardner seducing her brother, Clark Gable, in *Mogambo*.

JF Aranda in *Seeing in the Dark: A Compendium of Cinemagoing*

MOVIES BY NUMBERS

It Happened One Night (1934)
The Two Jakes (1990)
¡Three Amigos! (1986)
The Four Seasons (1981)
Five Easy Pieces (1970)
Six Degrees of Separation (1993)
The Seven Samurai (1954)
8MM (1999)
Nine to Five (1980)
The Ten Commandments (1956)

Number of computer effects technicians who worked on The Lord of 145
the Rings *trilogy*

MOVIE DOUBLE ACTS

Laurel and Hardy

Stan Laurel (1890–1965)
Laurel suffered a nervous breakdown on the death of Oliver Hardy and according to his friends, never fully recovered. He appears on sleeve of The Beatles' 'Sgt Pepper's Lonely Hearts Club Band' album.

Oliver Hardy (1892–1957)
Hardy was in over 400 films. He can also be seen on the sleeve of The Beatles' 'Sgt Pepper's Lonely Hearts Club'.

He used Babe Hardy as a screen name, until he was convinced by a numerologist that the longer screen name, Oliver Hardy, would bring him success.

List of feature-length 'talkies' they appeared in together (they also appeared in many shorts and silent films together):

Pardon Us (1931)
Pack up Your Troubles (1932)
Sons of the Desert (1933)
Babes in Toyland (1934)
Bohemian Girl (1936)
Our Relations (1936)
Way Out West (1937)
Block-Heads (1938)
Swiss Miss (1938)
Flying Deuces (1939)
A Chump at Oxford (1940)
Saps at Sea (1940)

COUNTRIES WITH THE MOST CINEMA SCREENS

Country	No. of screens in 2001
China	65,500
USA	36,764
India	11,962
France	5,236
Germany	4,792
Spain	3,770
UK	3,248
Italy	3,050
Canada	2,900
Japan	2,585

146 *Type of Boeing 747 used in* Air Force One *(1997) to mimic the Boeing 747-200 used by the president. Paint work cost $300,000*

EXTRA, EXTRA

Film	Country	Year	Extras
1. *Gandhi*	UK	1982	294,560
2. *Kolberg*	Germany	1945	187,000
3. *Monster Wangmagwi*	South Korea	1967	157,000
4. *War and Peace*	USSR	1968	120,000
5. *Ilya Muromets*	USSR	1956	106,000
('The Sword and the Dragon')			
6. *Dun-Huang* (aka 'Ton ko')	Japan	1988	100,000
7. *Razboiul independentei*	Romania	1912	80,000
('The War of Independence')			
8. *Around the World*			
in 80 Days	US	1956	68,894
9. *Intolerance*	US	1916	60,000
9. *Dny Zrady*	Czechoslovakia	1973	60,000
('Days of Betrayal')			

Today films tend to use computer-created casts of extras, so *Gandhi* is unlikely to be toppled.

WORDS ON FILM

While I was in New York, a friend told me that he had witnessed the synchronization of sound in films and predicted that it would shortly revolutionise the whole film industry.

I did not think of it again until months later when the Warner Brothers produced their first talking sequence. It was a costume picture, showing a very lovely actress – who shall be nameless – emoting silently over some great sorrow, her big, soulful eyes imparting anguish beyond the eloquence of Shakespeare. Then suddenly a new element entered the film – the noise that one hears when putting a sea-shell to one's ear. Then the lovely princess spoke as though through sand: 'I shall marry Gregory, even at the cost of giving up the throne.' It was a terrible shock, for until then the princess had enthralled us. As the picture progressed the dialogue became funnier, but not as funny as the sound effects. When the handle of the boudoir door turned I thought someone had cranked up a farm tractor, and when the door closed it sounded like the collision of two lumber trucks. At the beginning they knew nothing about controlling sound: a knight-errant in armour clanged like the noise in a steel factory, a simple family dinner sounded like the rush hour at a cheap restaurant, and the pouring of water into a glass made a peculiar tone that ran up the scale to high C. I came away from the theatre believing the days of sound were numbered.

Charles Chaplin, *My Autobiography*

Number of small firecrackers attached to James Caan's body to simulate 147
his death in The Godfather (1972)

TAGLINE TEASERS

On which movie posters would you see these taglines?

1. Love means never having to say you're sorry.

2. Get ready for rush hour.

Answers on page 153.

FILMGOERS' FOLLIES

As film fans know to their cost, the magic of cinema is often destroyed by the wrong kind of audience. Here are some typical culprits:

The Inappropriate Laugher

The person who snorts loudly not at the punch line, along with the rest of the audience, but at random moments in the film that are not the least bit funny. The culprit is usually a film buff pretending that there are jokes in the script that only they can understand.

The Eater

The person who brings in food that should not be tackled in a cinema, like triple-wrapped sweets or spaghetti bolognese. They eat throughout the film, delving noisily into a bottomless bag of snacks, offering each item in turn to the five embarrassed friends they brought with them. Involves a lot of rustling, munching and whispering.

The Prolific Pee-er

The person who, despite knowing they possess a small bladder, nevertheless buys a super-size soft drink and deliberately sits in the centre of the row, and then steps on your feet every one of the several times they have to get up to go to the toilet.

The Too Important

The person who not only leaves their phone on, but also answers it if it rings and then actually conducts a conversation. The recommended course of action is to wrestle the phone from their miserable hands and drop it in a 24oz cup of Coca-Cola.

The Snoggers

Teenagers with nowhere else to go who are too inconsiderate to sit in the back row, thus forcing everyone else to watch them snog in silhouette.

The Sleeper

The person who forgets that they missed their afternoon nap and has it in the cinema instead. Will snore intermittently throughout the film, especially at tense or romantic moments.

The Confused

Unable to follow even a simple plot, this person asks their companion in a loud whisper to explain it to them approximately every five minutes. For example: 'What are they doing?' 'What did he say?' and 'Why doesn't she just shoot him?' A good question.

Movie-making is the process of turning money into light. All they have at the end of the day is images flickering on a wall.
John Boorman, British director, *Money into Light*

CRINGING OSCAR MOMENTS

In 1998 Gwyneth Paltrow won best actress for *Shakespeare in Love*, and told the world: 'I would not have been able to play this role had I not understood love with a tremendous magnitude.' She also thanked several dead relatives. She broke down in tears and was subsequently ridiculed for her outburst.

Before Oscar winners were forced off the stage by an orchestra working by the clock, Greer Garson spent at least five minutes at the podium in 1942 after winning best actress for *Mrs Miniver*, although legend has managed to swell her stint to over an hour. The time limit was introduced soon after her epic list of thanks.

Having never been awarded an Oscar for an individual film,

Alfred Hitchcock was presented with a lifetime achievement award in 1967, in recognition of his hugely influential career. The audience awaited a witty and offbeat speech to match his television and after dinner performances but were disappointed when he shuffled on stage, muttered 'thank you' and walked slowly off stage back to his seat.

In 1978 Vanessa Redgrave used her acceptance speech for best supporting actress for *Julia* as a diatribe against 'Zionist hoodlums'. Dozens of police officers had to quell a protest outside the theatre. Playwright Paddy Chayefsky, who followed her onstage, quipped, 'A simple "thank you" would have been sufficient.'

COMIC BOOK FILMS

Film	Original comic book characters by
Dick Tracy (1990)	Chester Gould
Batman (1989)	Bob Kane
The Crow (1994)	James O'Barr
Ghost World (2000)	Daniel Clowes
Hulk (2003)	Stan Lee and Jack Kirby
Spider-Man (2002)	Stan Lee and Steve Ditko
Superman (1978)	Jerry Siegel and Joe Shuster
Teenage Mutant Ninja Turtles (1990)	Kevin Eastman and Peter Laird
X-Men (2000)	Stan Lee

TOP TEN WORST ACCENTS

1. Sean Connery in *The Untouchables* (1987) trying to be Irish
2. Dick Van Dyke in *Mary Poppins* (1964) trying to be Cockney
3. Brad Pitt in *Seven Years in Tibet* (1997) trying to be Austrian
4. Charlton Heston in *Touch of Evil* (1958) trying to be Mexican
5. Heather Graham in *From Hell* (2001) trying to be English
6. Keanu Reeves in *Bram Stoker's Dracula* (1992) trying to be English
7. Julia Roberts in *Mary Reilly* (1996) trying to be Irish
8. Laurence Olivier in *The Jazz Singer* (1980) trying to be 'end of the pier Jewish'
9. Pete Postlethwaite in *The Usual Suspects* (1995) trying to be Indian
10. Meryl Streep in *Out of Africa* (1985) trying to be Danish

Sean Connery has a special place in the film accent Hall of Shame. Here is a quick look at some of his worst moments.

Film	Trying to be...	Sounds...
Highlander (1986)	Spanish	Scottish
The Hunt for Red October (1990)	Russian	Scottish
The Untouchables (1987)	Irish	Scottish
First Knight (1995)	English	Scottish

FILM JOBS YOU'VE NEVER UNDERSTOOD

Best Boy – Assistant to the gaffer. This term was probably taken from early sailing and whaling crews, as sailors were often employed to set up and work rigging in theatres. There are no 'best girls' *per se;* female assistants are also called 'Best Boys.'

Foley Artist – The person who creates sound effects. Named after Jack Foley, an early practitioner of the art form.

Gaffer – The chief lighting technician/electrician for a production who is in charge of the electrical department and so the supplying, placing and maintenance of the lights on set. In the sixteenth century. 'gaffer' denoted a man who was the head of any organised group of labourers.

Greensman – Crew member who buys, places, and maintains any vegetation on a set.

Swing Gang – A group that is responsible for constructing and taking down a set.

Dolly Grip – The dolly is a small truck that rolls along tracks and carries the camera. It also carries part of the camera crew and perhaps the director. The dolly grip moves this equipment.

Key Grip – The chief grip works directly with the gaffer to create shadow effects for set lighting. They also supervise the transporting and setting up of equipment and the pushing of the dolly according to the requirements of the director of photography.

Leadman – The leadman is in charge of the swing gang and the set dressers.

DURING THE COMPILATION OF THIS BOOK, THE COMPANION TEAM...

Watched 293 films

Perfected the Bollywood Bhangra, but still couldn't flashdance

Spent 18.3 hours choosing which film to watch from the video shop

Saw films in eight different languages

Forgot their glasses twice so they couldn't read the subtitles

Built the Titanic from their desks, stood on top, forgot what they started out to do and sang 'The Hills Are Alive' instead

Consumed 3,115 pieces of popcorn, 459 nachos, 27 cola-related products, and by mistake three cinema tickets in one night alone

Fell asleep on the sofa before the end of a film 12 times

Left three umbrellas, two sets of keys and four overdue videos under seats at the cinema

Fell asleep at their desk nine times in the office having stayed up all night to watch the Oscars

Wrote four versions of their own Oscar speech, one unfinished due to sleep deprivation

Realised the following morning that the nachos were also a mistake

Please note that although every effort has been made to ensure accuracy in this book, the above statistics may be the result of dimly-lit minds.

Cinema is an old whore, like circus and variety, who knows how to give many kinds of pleasure.

Fedérico Fellini

MIXED-UP MOVIE STARS AND TAGLINE TEASERS

The answers. As if you needed them.

P11. 1. *Being John Malkovich* (1999)
      2. *The Hunt for Red October* (1990)

P23. 1. *Single White Female* (1992)
      2. *Alien* (1979)

P27. Uma Thurman, Robin Williams and Rowan Atkinson

P39. 1. *Indiana Jones and the Last Crusade* (1989)
      2. *A Clockwork Orange* (1971)

P48. 1. *LA Confidential* (1997)
      2. *Fight Club* (1999)

P53. 1. *A Fish Called Wanda* (1988)
      2. *Platoon* (1986)

P58. Andie MacDowell, Clint Eastwood and Arnold Swarzenegger

P68. 1. *The Silence of the Lambs* (1991)
      2. *When Harry Met Sally...* (1989)

P76. Robert de Niro, Tom Cruise and Elizabeth Taylor

P84. Burt Reynolds, Danny De Vito and Sigourney Weaver

P90. Sylvester Stallone, Emma Thompson and Gerard Depardieu

P105. Drew Barrymore, Michael Caine and Pierce Brosnan

P107. Meg Ryan, Gary Oldman and Winona Ryder

P115. Mel Gibson, Sean Connery and Demi Moore

P124. 1. *Shakespeare in Love* (1998)
      2. *Predator* (1987)

P137. Kenneth Branagh, Kim Basinger and Al Pacino

P143. 1. *Reservoir Dogs* (1992)
      2. *The Truman Show* (1998)

P148. 1. *Love Story* (1970)
      2. *Speed* (1994)

JOTTINGS IN THE DARK

The Top Ten of Everything 2004, Russell Ash

The Top 10 of Film, Russell Ash

Amazing Animal Actors, Pauline C Bartel

The Complete Hitchcock, Paul Condon

Marilyn: In Her Own Words, compiled by Neil Grant

Cinemas in Britain, 100 Years of Cinema Architecture, Richard Gray

Celebrity feuds!: The Cattiest Rows, Spats, and Tiffs Ever Recorded, Boze Hadleigh

The Universal Story, Clive Hirschhorn

Warner Brothers Story, Clive Hirschhorn

The Disney Villain, Ollie Johnston

Not So Dumb: Animals in the Movies, Raymond Lee

Time Out Film Guide, John Pym

Film Facts, Patrick Robertson

Hollywood Cocktails, Tobias Steed

Guinness Box Office Hits: No 1 Movie Hits in the UK, Phil Swern

The Celebrity Lists Book, Mitchell Symons

Bollywood Dreams, Jonathan Torgovnik

ACKNOWLEDGEMENTS

We gratefully acknowledge permission to reprint extracts of copyright material in this book from the following authors, publishers and executors:

The Deeper Meaning of Liff, Douglas Adams and John Lloyd by kind permission of ED Victor Ltd.

Conversations with Jack Cardiff: Art, light and direction in Cinema, Justin Bowyer by kind permission of Chysalis Books Group PLC.

Seeing in the Dark: A Compendium of Cinema Going, Ian Breakwell (Ed) and Paul Hammond (Ed) by kind permission of Serpentstail.

From *A Clockwork Orange* by Anthony Burgess (c) The Estate of Anthony Burgess, by arrangement with Artellus Limited.

Breakfast at Tiffany's by Truman Capote published by Penguin Books. Used by permission of The Random House Group Limited

I am Jackie Chan – My Life in Action, Jackie Chan by kind permission of Pan Macmillan.

Extract from *My Autobiography* by Charles Chaplin published by Bodley Head. Used by permission of The Random House Group Limited.

Future Indefinite by Noël Coward, published by Methuen Publishing Ltd. Copyright (c) The Estate of Noël Coward

Extract from *Tony Curtis: The Autobiography* by Tony Curtis and Barry Paris published by William Heinemann. Used by permission of The Random House Group Limited.

My Story, Ava Gardner by kind permission of Random House Group Limited.

198 words from *The Family At One End Street* by Eve Garnett (Puffin Modern Classics, 1942), Copyright © Eve Garnett, 1942

Approximately 200 words from *A Positively Final Appearance* by Alec Guinness (Hamish Hamilton, 1999) Copyright © Alec Guinness, 1999.

Brave New World, Aldous Huxley by kind permission of The Reece Halsey Agency.

Extract from *My Lucky Stars* by Shirley MacLaine published by Bantam Press. Used by permission of Random House Group Limited.

INDEX

The Cook's Companion
Whether your taste is for foie gras or fry-ups, this tasty compilation is an essential ingredient in any kitchen, boiling over with foodie facts, fiction, science, history and trivia.
ISBN 1-86105-772-5

The Gardener's Companion
For anyone who has ever put on a pair of gloves, picked up a spade and gone out into the garden in search of flowers, beauty and inspiration.
ISBN 1-86105-771-7

The Literary Companion
Whether your Dickens is Charles or Monica, your Stein Gertrude or Franken, this is the book for you. The full range of literary fact and fiction from Rebecca East to Vita Sackville-West.
ISBN 1-86105-798-9

The London Companion
From Edgware to Morden, Upminster to Ealing, here's your chance to explore the history, mystery and many peculiarities of the most exciting capital city in the world.
ISBN 1-86105-799-7

The Politics Companion
The history, myths, great leaders and greater liars of international politics are all gathered around the hustings in this remarkable compilation. This is the book that finally makes politics tick.
ISBN 1-86105-796-2

The Traveller's Companion
For anyone who's ever stared at a distant plane, wondered where it's going, and spent the rest of the day dreaming of faraway lands and ignoring everything and everyone else.
ISBN 1-86105-773-3

The Walker's Companion
If you've ever laced a sturdy boot, packed a cheese and pickle sandwich, and put one foot in front of the other in search of stimulation and contemplation, then this book is for you.
ISBN 1-86105-825-X

The Wildlife Companion
Animal amazements, ornithological oddities and botanical beauties abound in this compilation of natural need-to-knows and nonsense for wildlife-lovers everywhere.
ISBN 1-86105-770-9